MANDATE *for* MERCY

A Call to Compassionate Action for a Hurting World

DON STEPHENS

ywam
PUBLISHING
A MINISTRY OF YOUTH WITH A MISSION
P.O. Box 55787, Seattle, WA 98155

YWAM Publishing is the publishing ministry of Youth With A Mission. Youth With A Mission (YWAM) is an international missionary organization of Christians from many denominations dedicated to presenting Jesus Christ to this generation. To this end, YWAM has focused it's efforts in three main areas: 1) Training and equipping believers for their part in fulfilling the Great Commission (Matthew 28:19). 2) Personal evangelism. 3) Mercy ministry (medical and relief work).

For a free catalog of books and materials write or call:

YWAM Publishing
P.O. Box 55787, Seattle, WA 98155
(206)771-1153 or (800) 922-2143

Mandate for Mercy

Published by Youth With A Mission Publishing
P.O. Box 55787, Seattle, WA 98155, USA.

Unless noted other wise, all Scripture quotations are taken from the HOLY BIBLE, NEW INTERNATIONAL VERSION, Copyright © 1973, 1978, 1984 by the International Bible Society. Used by permission of Zondervan Bible Publishers.

ISBN 0-927545-81-0

Printed in the United States of America.

Dedicated to the thousands of faithful men and women who have selflessly served with Mercy Ships. Your compassion has been inspiring, and the results eternal. And to my YWAM family, who dared to believe in a dream, and willingly sacrificed to make it reality.

The quality of mercy is not strained,
It droppeth as the gentle rain from heaven
Upon the place beneath: it is twice blessed;
It blesseth him that gives and him that takes:

It is enthronèd in the hearts of kings,
It is an attribute to God himself,
And earthly power doth then show likest God's
When mercy seasons justice.

The Merchant of Venice
William Shakespeare

Table of Contents

Introduction

THE THUD OF THE ROPE LADDER against the side of the ship woke me. I fumbled for my watch: it was 4:00 a.m. It must be the pilot coming aboard to guide the ship into the harbor and to her berth.

I threw some clothes on and quickly made my way up on deck. Sure enough, we were just passing under the Sunshine Skyway Bridge into Tampa Bay. Standing on deck, I felt the fresh sea breeze against my face. As the lights of St. Petersburg and then Tampa came into view, a surge of gratitude pulsed through me.

Awed, I contemplated all God had done to make Mercy Ships a reality—the committed crew, the faithful supporters, and the lives that had been touched in so many practical ways. As I praised the Lord, I thanked Him for His guidance in securing this vessel, a retired Norwegian coastal ferry. A rugged, seaworthy ship with a reasonably shallow draft, she was perfect for the Caribbean where we planned to use her. Newly christened the *Caribbean Mercy*, she was the fourth in our fleet of mercy ships, joining the *Anastasis*, the *Island Mercy*, and the *Pacific Ruby*.

Four mercy ships. Yes! But we've hardly scratched the surface of ministering to the poor, the needy, and the hurting of this world. Much more needs to be done.

Sometimes I can be overwhelmed with all the needs—at those times I must remind myself that no person or group of people can do it alone. Meeting the needs of the poor and needy in Jesus' name is the responsibility of all Christians.

The statistics on suffering in our world are almost unbelievable. Every day 30,000 children die from drinking contaminated water and from a lack of basic sanitation, 10,000 people die from a lack of vaccinations, and 35,000 people starve to death.

The list could go on, but the figures become numbing, almost incomprehensible after a while. The scope of suffering in our world is truly staggering.

But what can we do about it? That is the vexing question.

Indeed, most human beings have suffering as their traveling companion at some point in their lives. But some people, most notably those in developing world countries, seem to bear a disproportionate amount of suffering.

As Christians, though, we can play an important role in the lives of those who suffer.

My mother is a very practical Christian woman. As I grew up, she instilled in me the notion of what I have termed the "two-handed" Gospel: One hand offers practical concern and help, and the other offers spiritual care and guidance. My mother looked out for people's physical *and* spiritual well-being. She was always doing practical little things for people to let them know someone cared about them and wanted to help them bear any suffering they may be experiencing.

Mercy Ships is founded upon the ideal of the "two-handed" Gospel. We are concerned about people's physical *and* spiritual needs. It's not enough simply to offer to meet a person's physical need without spending equal time addressing his spiritual needs. And neither is it enough to address the spiritual needs and pay no attention to the physical needs.

No, the "two-handed" Gospel is a straightforward and practical approach drawn directly from the pages of the Bible and from the life of Jesus. Jesus lived His life to minister to both the physical and spiritual needs of the people He came in contact with. And He spent much time admonishing and encouraging His followers to do the same.

When most Christians read through the gospels, I think they recognize immediately the contours of the "two-handed" Gospel, though they may call it by some other name. With God's help we must strive to practice it if we are truly to make an impact on our world, our nations, and our societies with the life-changing claims of Jesus Christ.

This book is a challenge to all of us who want to change our world with the message of the Gospel. It is not a treatise on mercy and compassion; it is a mandate— a *mandate for mercy.* It is a challenge to minister to the physical and spiritual needs of people wherever we find them, be it in our own street, in our own city or nation, or on the other side of the globe in some developing world nation.

The question is: Are we up for the challenge?

Chapter One

❧❧

Seeing the World
Through Different Eyes

❧❧

THE SKY IS STILL OVERCAST but the rain has stopped and people are beginning to come out in the open. Although they have survived the disaster, there is no joy. The ground is littered with splintered trees, the remains of family homes, and personal belongings. Through the debris the survivors wander, shoulders down, holding on to one another for comfort. But it is their eyes that tell the depth of the tragedy.

The eyes of the young hold amazement while the older eyes are shadowed with grief and despair. They know how much work went into building these homes. Now all they can see is destruction. Everyone is suffering and no one is there to lend a hand.

It could be anywhere. We've seen the images from Bangladesh, where 100,000 people died in a typhoon. In

Africa, millions fled to Zaire from the war in Rwanda. We saw the devastation in southern Florida after Hurricane Andrew, and in California after the Loma Prieta earthquake. The debris is different, the skin color changes, but the eyes are the same.

We watch our television sets, read magazines and newspapers, and the images keep coming. How do we respond? How do we interpret what we see?

Answers vary greatly. Some of us will respond with a great deal of indifference, others with deep concern. Some will be led to take action, others will choose to continue in inaction. But regardless of how we respond, this one thing is true: In large part our response has been shaped by the culture that surrounded us as we grew up.

While growing up, we absorb certain values from the culture around us, and in turn, these create a broad system—a world view—whereby we analyze things that occur in the world, and by which we determine how we should respond to the suffering we see. If I had been born and raised in Hindu India, I would have formulated a very different world view than the one I formulated being raised by Christian parents in Colorado.

These world views can be compared to eyeglasses through which we see things. Our families, schools, churches, beliefs, and political affiliations all contribute to the refractive characteristics of the lenses in our glasses. And while these glasses fall into broad cultural categories, they nonetheless create a unique and individual view of the world for the person wearing them.

Interestingly, we become so used to wearing our cultural glasses that we forget they're there. We assume everyone else is looking through the same lenses as we are. So the way we view things becomes the way things are, or the way we think they ought to be.

But the way we think things *ought* to be is not necessarily the way things *should* be. Not all world views are equal. Not all world views, regardless of their cultural and historical underpinnings, are based upon truths that account adequately for the way things are in our world. Nowhere are these differences more apparent than in interpreting and responding to suffering.

When it comes to how people respond to suffering, their responses fall into four basic and broad world-view categories.

The first category I call the *fatalistic world view.* This world view is shaped by the thinking and tenets of eastern religion. In this view, things are the way they are because that is the way they are meant to be. People looking through these cultural glasses at the devastation in Bangladesh would say to themselves, "What will be will be. God is in charge, and He has chosen to visit these people with affliction for reasons only He is aware of. This was meant to happen to the people of Bangladesh."

The second category is the *karmic world view.* This view is also shaped by eastern religion. Karma can be good or bad, and according to this view, each individual is in a state of cosmic flux moving up or down the ladder of endless cycles of life, depending upon that person's karma.

If the person's karma is good, the next life will be one more rung up the ladder that leads to Nirvana—the cessation of existence. However, if a person's karma is bad, the next life will be a rung lower on the ladder, and bad things will happen to the person. When these people view southern Florida, they say to themselves, "That hurricane hit those people because they have earned it by their actions in a previous life. They had bad karma."

The third category is the *analytic world view.* This

view is formed by western rationalism and scientism. According to this view, suffering is a result of the uneven distribution of wealth and resources. People who hold to this view study historic context and other factors to try and understand how this inequity in the distribution of resources has occurred and how it can be overcome. So they look at California after the earthquake and say, "We have a problem. We need to study and find out why this happened. We need to build better bridges. We need better emergency services. We must study earthquakes so we can warn people and ensure that such a catastrophe doesn't happen to these people again."

These first three world views may seem very different, but they share one thing in common—they are closed systems where man is the measure of all things. No personal God is interested in mankind's plight, so when faced with suffering, men and women must simply accept it, and in the case of the analytic world view, through human effort try and limit the impact future catastrophes have on people. Within closed systems, an immediate compassionate response to those who are suffering is not mandated.

At first glance, the analytic world view may seem to be very compassionate, but in fact, its real focus of concern is ensuring that the same misfortune does not affect others. In the process, immediate and compassionate actions are displaced by good intentions for the future.

Then there is a fourth world view, which also determines how we view and respond to suffering around us. This world view was illuminated for us by Jesus in one of His parables. His parable, though, was not about a village in Bangladesh, but about a man traveling a quiet road, minding his own business, who was attacked, robbed, and left for dead. Doubtless most of us remember the parable; it is probably the most well-known story Jesus ever told.

On one occasion an expert in the law stood up to test Jesus. "Teacher," he asked, "what must I do to inherit eternal life?"

"What is written in the Law?" he replied. "How do you read it?"

He answered: "'Love the Lord your God with all your heart and with all your soul and with all your strength and with all your mind'; and, 'Love your neighbor as yourself.'"

"You have answered correctly," Jesus replied. "Do this and you will live."

But he wanted to justify himself, so he asked Jesus, "And who is my neighbor?"

In reply Jesus said: "A man was going down from Jerusalem to Jericho, when he fell into the hands of robbers. They stripped him of his clothes, beat him and went away, leaving him half dead. A priest happened to be going down the same road, and when he saw the man, he passed by on the other side. So too, a Levite, when he came to the place and saw him, passed by on the other side. But a Samaritan, as he traveled, came where the man was; and when he saw him, he took pity on him. He went to him and bandaged his wounds, pouring on oil and wine. Then he put the man on his own donkey, took him to an inn and took care of him. The next day he took out two silver coins and gave them to the innkeeper. 'Look after him,' he said, 'and when I return, I will reimburse you for any extra expense you may have.'

"Which of these three do you think was a neighbor to the man who fell into the hands of robbers?"

The expert in the law replied, "The one who had mercy on him."

Jesus told him, "Go and do likewise."

Luke 10:25-37

This Samaritan man embodies the *Christo-centric world view*. It is a view that values the individual as important to God. Because people are important to Him, they should also be important to His followers. So whatever situation we may find people in, we are compelled to respond to them and their situation compassionately and swiftly, because we are His followers. We are, as the Scriptures direct, to love our neighbor as ourselves.

This Christo-centric world view stands at odds with all other world views. It is an open, not a closed system. It is a system that allows for a personal God to become involved with the needy through the lives of men and women, and to help them deal with and overcome suffering.

In this respect, Christianity is unique. It is the only religion that has mercy coupled with action as one of its foundation stones. And the story of the Good Samaritan illustrates what should happen when Christians are confronted with the suffering and needs of others.

It is also why a frail, octogenarian nun of Albanian descent is recognized as the champion of the poor and the outcast in India. When Mother Teresa walks the streets of Calcutta, she sees with the eyes of Jesus—eyes of mercy and compassion, with dignity for all human life.

The way Mother Teresa sees and responds to need stands in stark contrast to the way most in India, steeped in their fatalistic and karmic world views, see things. While they see people who deserve their misfortune because of fate or bad karma, Mother Teresa sees people who are loved by God and who desperately need to experience His touch in their lives.

Many others down through Church history have seen with those same eyes, too, and have acted accordingly. William Wilberforce was a prominent British politician in the early 1800s. After his conversion to Christianity he set about exposing the horrors of slavery and calling for laws to banish it from England. Largely due to his efforts, slavery came to be seen for the evil it is. Florence Nightingale, against the conventional wisdom of the day, gathered and trained the first group of female nurses to tend the wounded during the Crimean War. William Booth, seeing orphaned and neglected children on the streets of London, vowed to do something to help them. The result was the establishment of the Salvation Army. Elizabeth Fry championed prison reform in Europe during the nineteenth century. Thanks to her efforts, significant changes were made in the way prisoners and the insane were treated.

The list could go on, but the point is this: A single thread runs through the lives of all these people—they were courageous, and they were committed because they were Christians. Indeed, it would have been odd for them to do what they did if they had not been Christians, given Christianity's emphasis on compassion for our fellow man.

Of course, the Lord Jesus Himself provides the most vivid picture of what it means to live a life full of mercy and compassion for other people. Even when His compassion cut against the traditional way of doing things, He carried on. He healed a man with a crippled hand on the Sabbath; He counseled a despised Samaritan woman; He dined with and ministered to tax collectors and prostitutes alike. His behavior pushed people to think through what they really believed. Were their beliefs truly based upon God's truth?

And not only did Jesus live this way, He admonished His disciples to do the same!

> Give to everyone who asks you, and if anyone takes what belongs to you, do not demand it back. Do to others as you would have them do to you. If you love those who love you, what credit is that to you? Even "sinners" love those who love them. And if you do good to those who are good to you, what credit is that to you? Even "sinners" do that. And if you lend to those from whom you expect repayment, what credit is that to you? Even "sinners" lend to "sinners," expecting to be repaid in full. But love your enemies, do good to them, and lend to them without expecting to get anything back. Then your reward will be great, and you will be sons of the Most High, because he is kind to the ungrateful and wicked. *Be merciful, just as your Father is merciful.* [Italics mine.]
>
> Luke 6:30-36

Why mercy and compassion? Why did Jesus spend so much of His time instilling in His followers the need for them to be compassionate and merciful?

The answer to the first question is obvious: God is a God of mercy and compassion. To be His follower is to be a person of mercy and compassion. But there is a second reason: In reaching out to people with mercy and compassion, we present them with behavior they cannot easily account for in their world view. We "gate crash" their presuppositions. We don't play by their rules.

Remember the story of the woman at the well? The disciples had left Jesus at the well when they went to buy some food, and a woman came to the well to draw water. The fact that Jesus would even talk to her totally disarmed her. He was a Jew; she was a despised Samaritan. She was from an ordered, closed society where everybody knew their place. The simple act of Jesus talking to her and asking her to draw water for Him threw her world view into disarray. At that point, Jesus had her complete attention and was able to address deeper issues in her life.

In the same way, acts of mercy—be they offering medical care, building water treatment systems, constructing houses, or teaching the importance of hygiene—challenge the way people have been taught to think about themselves and the situations in which they find themselves.

When we treat needy persons with kindness, mercy, and compassion, hope is kindled within them. Maybe there is a different way for them to look at themselves and their situation. Perhaps there is hope for them to overcome their situation. Maybe their circumstances will not suffocate them. Perhaps there is new meaning and a new path for their life. Maybe God has a destiny for their life.

I heard a report recently from an outreach group that had been working among the Hmong, a Buddhist people group in Thailand. Just before the group had arrived, three newborn babies died of tetanus. The deaths were accepted fatalistically by the Hmong—the babies were obviously destined to die. Beyond that, the Hmong did not question why the deaths had occurred or if there were any way to prevent further deaths.

When the outreach team arrived and heard of the deaths, the nurse was determined to get to the bottom of the matter. She investigated and found that rather than fate, the cause of the deaths had been the rusty knife the midwife used to cut the umbilical chords of the newborn babies. Eventually she convinced the midwife to use a clean surgical knife to cut the cords, and to sterilize the knife after each use. As a result, lives were saved. No more newborn babies died of tetanus.

Something as simple as teaching a midwife to use a clean knife to cut a baby's umbilical cord challenged the fatalistic world view of that Hmong village. That nurse had shown them they didn't have to accept things as fate; they could change the outcome of events. And more importantly, the door was opened for them to see that there was a God who was really interested in them, and who could, in fact, change the outcome of their lives.

John Mbiti, a philosopher and theologian from Kenya, has done extensive research on 270 different language groups in Africa (not dialects, but entirely separate language groups). In all 270 language groups he has not found a single word for "future." Each of those 270 language groups reflects a culture that does not see the events of life as moving forward, but rather as moving in cycles. There are the cycles of the rainy season and the dry season, birth and death, planting and reaping. Since everything moves in cycles, there is no real future, just cyclic toil. So there is no real need for a word to convey such a concept as "future." And the absence of such a concept ties the people to their cyclic, fatalistic world view.

How different is the Christian world view! For Christians, history is going somewhere. We draw from the past, build in the present, and plan for the future. The very first words recorded in the Bible are, "In the beginning God..." (Genesis 1:1). At the beginning of the world, God was there orchestrating events. And right at the end of the Bible in Revelation 22:20 we read, "'Yes, I am coming soon.' Amen. Come, Lord Jesus."

This is the future hope of every Christian!

The essence of the Gospel is that we have a beginning, we were created, and the decisions we make during our life will affect our future. The Gospel also speaks of God redeeming our past, becoming an active partner with us in this life, and securing for us a future hope.

It is simple and wonderful. It is what marks Christianity as unique from all other world views. And one of the most effective ways I know to bring people face to face with the truth of the Gospel and the Christian world view is through simple acts of mercy and kindness.

Getting Our Focus Right

When Jesus told the story of the Good Samaritan, He meant it to be both an illustration of what it means as a Christian to practice mercy, and as a rebuke to the religious people of the day. The way of mercy that Jesus pointed out in His parable was not an unknown concept to the Jews; mercy is a theme that runs deep throughout the Old Testament. The Jews were admonished to take care of the poor and the needy, the orphans and the widows, the sick and the dying, and not just among their own. They were also instructed to show mercy and kindness to strangers. But over the years, the necessity of mercy had grown dim in their minds. That is why the characters in Jesus' story are so important: a priest, a

Levite, and a Samaritan.

The priest and the Levite represented the Jews: both served in the temple, both were schooled in the Scriptures. They should have known better than to pass by the beaten man on the other side of the road. They should have been the first to offer help, but they didn't. It was left to a Samaritan, whom the Jews despised for their aberrant religious beliefs, to do what the priest and the Levite should have done.

The parable of the Good Samaritan is a stinging rebuke to the Jews for their lack of mercy and compassion. But in the Church today, we have become like those Jews Jesus rebuked. We have allowed mercy and compassion to grow dim in our midst. We have focused too much on ourselves and our spiritual and material needs, and have closed our hearts and hands to the poor and the needy around us.

That is why I have written this book. My purpose is not to rebuke, but to challenge. In the pages that follow, I want to challenge Christians everywhere to once again renew their commitment to mercy and compassion. I want to challenge the Church to rise up and, through mercy, challenge the people of this world with the life-changing power of the Gospel.

I have experienced firsthand how mercy, given in the name of the Lord Jesus, can change people and societies, even in the midst of catastrophe. My prayer in writing this book is that you may come to experience this firsthand, too.

Chapter Two

Echoes of Mercy

They will be hushed by a good deed who laugh at a wise speech. —French Proverb

IRIS LIVED WITH HER HUSBAND and three children in a one-room thatched shack in a slum area of Barahona in the Dominican Republic. She became pregnant again, and had no idea she was having twins until they actually arrived—one boy and one girl.

It should have been a time of rejoicing, but it wasn't, because the twins were so different. They may have been nurtured in the same womb, but that is where the similarity ended. James was a handsome, strong, curly-haired baby boy. Wanda, on the other hand, was small and weak. She also had a cleft palate which split the inside of her mouth from her nose through her upper lip.

Privately, Iris' neighbors thought she should just leave the girl to die and be glad providence had given her at least one healthy child. But Iris' maternal instincts were strong, and she decided to fight for the life of her newborn daughter.

She set about trying to find the medical help Wanda needed. But the family had no real source of income, and soon what little money they did have was exhausted. Once the money was gone, there seemed little else Iris could do.

Because of the cleft palate, it was almost impossible to feed Wanda, and she succumbed quickly to the effects of malnutrition. All Iris could do was sit and wait for the inevitable—Wanda's death.

With a sadness only a mother could know, Iris watched her son thrive and grow stronger, while Wanda began to lose her fragile grip on life. Then she heard some wonderful news. A hospital ship had docked just ten minutes away from Barahona. Quickly, she wrapped Wanda in clean rags and set out for the nearby screening station the ship had set up.

When the screening nurses unwrapped the rags, they exchanged knowing looks. It was probably too late for this baby. She was so malnourished that even if they could save her life, she'd surely have extensive brain damage.

Quietly, they discussed their options. Even though the situation seemed hopeless for Wanda, they had to do something, and do it right away, even before the ship's hospital was ready to admit patients.

Within a matter of minutes, Iris and her child were escorted directly to our hospital ship, the *Anastasis,* where American nurse Diedre Graham took the first shift giving Wanda the intensive assistance she needed. Wanda was placed into an intensive care incubator. As the first day rolled into the next, many nurses, as well as members of the ship's evangelism team, stopped by to offer encouragement and to tell Iris about God's love for her and her child.

Iris appreciated their words of encouragement and comfort, but she was deeply touched by the actions of the medical team as they cared for Wanda in her life-or-death struggle. Even after making it clear she had no money to pay for Wanda's care, they gave the same level of care as before.

For a while, Wanda seemed to stabilize, but forty-eight hours after being admitted to the ship's hospital, she lost her battle and died peacefully.

Diedre removed the tubes from the little body and comforted Iris. And that day, as Iris struggled with her feelings over the death of her daughter, she reached out and asked Jesus to come into her life and fill her with His peace.

When Iris returned home with Wanda's body, the neighbors were fearful for her mental state. They knew how much she'd loved her daughter, and how hard she'd tried to save the girl's life, and they thought the strain of the death might be too much for Iris to bear.

But although Iris grieved, she had found hope. She told her neighbors about the ship, and the people who gave what they had without extracting money or promises first. She told them about trained foreign medical personnel who sat through the night to monitor Wanda. And she told them about the God of love and mercy she had heard about, and how she had accepted Him into her heart.

The news of what the crew of the *Anastasis* had done to try to save Wanda's life soon spread throughout the village—as well as the news that Iris had become a Christian.

The next Tuesday evening, when Diedre Graham

and several crew members from the *Anastasis* came to visit Iris and conduct a Bible study, they found that her neighbors hung around outside. And the following Tuesday evening, the neighbors asked if they could stay and listen, too.

By the time the *Anastasis* sailed from Barahona two months later, Iris was conducting the Tuesday night Bible study herself, and Diedre had put the core group of 15 women in touch with a nearby pastor, who welcomed them into his church.

Some would say that the story of baby Wanda is one of defeat. For the first time in Mercy Ships' history the medical crew had failed to save the life of someone in their care.

Yet Iris and those in her community had learned through their harsh lives that not every story has a happy ending. What made an impact on them was the efforts to try and save Wanda's life. As a result of the mercy shown to a mother and her dying child, there is a thriving group of Christians who meet together regularly to pray and study the Word of God in that slum in Barahona in the Dominican Republic.

Some may also question the point of trying to save the life of a child who in all probability would have had severe brain damage if she'd survived. But that is the spirit of the world speaking.

We Christians need to tune out the world's standards, and tune in to the voice of the God of all mercy. The choices of life and death are in His hands, not ours. There is a time to be born and a time to die, but we are not the ones to judge—He is.

Our call is to be bearers of His mercy to people in desperate need of it. And from firsthand experience, I have seen that whenever mercy is extended in Jesus' name it has an impact—no matter what the physical outcome may be.

Matthew's gospel tells how after being with Jesus for a time, the twelve disciples were sent out into the surrounding countryside to preach the Gospel. Before they left, Jesus gave them the following instructions:

> As you go, preach this message: "The king-dom of heaven is near." Heal the sick, raise the dead, cleanse those who have leprosy, drive out demons. Freely you have received, freely give.
>
> Matthew 10:7-8

In today's church the words, "Freely you have received, freely give," have become almost a cliché, caus-ing us to lose sight of some of their original impact. What the disciples had freely received they were to freely pass on to others.

And what was it they had so freely received?

No doubt the disciples felt they'd gained many things from their intensive training time with Jesus, but the most powerful was God's mercy and compassion.

From their checkered pasts, the disciples had been handpicked by the Son of God. They had walked and talked together. They had watched as Jesus reached out and touched people with a hand of mercy. They had seen Him heal the sick, raise the dead, cleanse lepers, and drive demons from people. And no doubt the disciples themselves had experienced Christ do similar things for them. Now they were to go out into the countryside and freely give to others what they had freely received from Jesus.

On another occasion, Jesus and the disciples crossed over the Sea of Galilee to where the Gerasenes lived. When they arrived, they encountered a deranged, demon-possessed man. Jesus cast the demons from the man, and we are told the man returned to his right mind.

However, Jesus' actions frightened those who had observed them, and they begged Him and His disciples to leave. As they climbed back into their boat, the formerly demon-possessed man wanted to go with them. But Jesus said no, and instead instructed him to, "Return home and tell how much God has done for you" (Luke 8:39).

That is exactly what the man did—he went far and wide throughout the land of the Gerasenes telling everyone he came in contact with what God had done for him. By freely testifying to what had been done for him, this man spread far and wide the impact of the act of mercy Jesus had performed for him.

Paul told the Corinthian Christians: "You show that you are a letter from Christ, the result of our ministry, written not with ink but with the Spirit of the living God, not on tablets of stone but on tablets of human hearts" (II Corinthians 3:3).

As Christians we are living embodiments of the mercy and forgiveness we have been shown. And as Paul gently reminded the Corinthians, people need to be able to read in our actions, not just in our words, that we have received these things from the Lord. Like all Christians before us, we are to be incarnations of the Gospel for our generation.

So the challenge is for us to be living testimonies for all to see, and giving freely to others from what we have received—forgiveness and mercy. We need to accurately portray to our world every facet of God's love and mercy.

Throughout Church history it has been the actions of Christians, rather than their words, which have made people receptive to embracing the Gospel message. In her book, *From Jerusalem to Irian Jaya,* Ruth Tucker points out that:

> Christianity penetrated the Roman world through five main avenues: the preaching and teaching of evangelists, the personal witness of believers, *acts of kindness and charity,* the faith shown in persecution and death, and the intellectual reasoning of the early apologists. [Italics mine.] [1]

Tucker also records a quote from Julian, fourth-century Roman Emperor. Although raised in a Christian environment, Julian had turned his back on Christianity in favor of classical paganism, whose influence he tried to reestablish in the Roman Empire. His efforts earned him the epithet, "The Apostate." In his attempts to undermine Christianity, Julian curtailed the rights and privileges granted to Christians by preceding emperors. His contempt for Christians was obvious by the name he called them—atheists. Yet despite his best efforts, he could not dislodge the Christian faith from the Empire or from people's hearts. In his frustration he wrote:

> Atheism [i.e., Christianity] has been specially advanced through the loving service rendered to strangers, and through their care for the burial of the dead. It is a scandal that there is not a single Jew who is a beggar, and that the godless Galileans [another of his derogatory terms for Christians] care not only for their own poor but for ours as well; while those who belong to us look in vain for the help that we should render them. [2]

What a charge these early Christians had leveled against them! Through offering mercy and kindness they were not only extending the kingdom of God, but also challenging leaders to face up to the shortcomings and inconsistencies of their own religious beliefs.

In his book, *The Spreading Flame,* F. F. Bruce records the following incident:

> When Alexandria was devastated by an outbreak of plague in the middle of the third century, Dionysius, bishop of the church in that city, describes the devotion with which Christians tended the sick, often catching the plague and dying of it themselves in consequence, whereas their pagan neighbors thrust from them those who showed the symptoms of plague and fled from their nearest and dearest. They would throw them into the streets half dead, or cast out their corpses without burial. [3]

And in discussing the growth and development of Christianity in tenth century Europe, noted Church historian Kenneth Scott Latourette observed:

> The Christian faith also stimulated care for the sick, the poor, and the stranger. In a society where strife was chronic and survival seemed to depend on ruthless struggle which had no use for the weak, monasteries regularly entertained travelers, parishes cared for the indigent, and in the name of Christ hospitals were founded and maintained for the ill and the aged. [4]

Such accounts led F. F. Bruce to conclude:

> When we try to account for the increase in the numbers of Christians in those days, in spite of official hostility, we must give due consideration to the impression that behavior of this kind would make on the pagan population. [5]

The early Christians were obviously known for acts of kindness and mercy, unlike other religious and philosophical groups of the time, who possessed many theories, but had little, if anything, to offer in the way of action. As a result, the echo of the compassionate and merciful acts of Christians reverberated through all levels of society, drawing people into the Church, and spreading Christianity through the then-known world.

✎Three Blind Men✎

When it comes to spreading the Gospel, often we Christians are like the proverbial three blind men with the elephant. Each man is asked to touch the elephant and then describe what it is like.

To the first man it is hard and cold, to the second, saggy and rough, and to the third, the elephant is thin and floppy. When they heard each other's descriptions, each thought the other was lying. But they weren't; it was just that the first man had felt the elephant's tusks, the second his belly, and the third his ears.

Likewise, some of us look at spreading the Gospel and say it's about preaching on street corners. Others say no, it's about witnessing to people in the work place. And still others say it's about running local church growth seminars.

While none of these is completely wrong, neither are they completely right. Spreading the Gospel involves each of them, and more. Spreading the message of salvation is an interconnected process that draws on many different facets and ministries within the Body of Christ.

In 1987, several thousand Christians were polled and asked what or who was primarily responsible for their conversion to Christ. Five percent said it was through an evangelistic crusade; 1-2% said it was through personal visitation in their home. Another 2-3% said their conversions were the result of deciding to attend church, and yet another 2-3% said their conversions were as a result of the program of a church in their area. About 4-5% came to the Lord through attending Sunday school, and 5-6% through talking with a pastor.

But a full 75-80% of those polled said it was through a friend or relative that they came to experience salvation, either through talking with the person, through the person's example, or both.

From the poll we can see the diversity of ways in which the Gospel is spread. However, one particular avenue stands out as being particularly more fruitful than the others. A person who has experienced the touch of God in his life, then shares about that incident with friends and family, has much greater impact in drawing a person into a relationship with the Lord than the other forms of witnessing and evangelizing.

An act of mercy, given in Jesus' name, can be the experience that gets a person talking to his friends and family about what he has experienced, in the same way that Iris told all her friends and neighbors in Barahona about what she had seen and experienced. Like the ever-widening circles on a pond after a stone has been thrown into it, the person's testimony spreads far and wide through his network of family, friends, and acquaintances.

🐾Open Doors🐾

Unfortunately, we late-twentieth-century Christians have lost sight of mercy as an important means of spreading the Gospel. In the minds of many—both Christians and non-Christians—mercy, compassion, and Christianity are no longer inseparable as they were for most of the Church's history. Rather, we tend to think of mercy in terms of its embodiment in particular individuals, Mother Teresa being a prime example.

However, the most cursory reading of the Bible reveals that God is filled with both mercy and compassion. Thus, while many of us may not be called to such a ministry of mercy like Mother Teresa's, each of us should embody the same spirit of mercy and compassion that she does. We all partake in the same Spirit of Christ, and His merciful and compassionate nature should show through in our lives.

Our world is no less needy today than it was at the time of the founding of the Church or during the dark ages of European history. Like then, mercy can break through cultural and ethnic barriers. It can cut through bitterness and hate, intolerance and injustice, ignorance and fear. Mercy can take the life-changing message of the Gospel into places where other forms of evangelism are barred. Too often we overrate people's objections to the Gospel message and underrate the desperation of their need.

The M/V *Anastasis* has spent time ministering in several countries which were predominantly Islamic. Before entering each of those countries, representatives from Mercy Ships talked to the government officials about how we have woven together the practical expression of the Gospel with the active proclamation of the message of salvation through Christ.

The first time we did this, I was very nervous. I had been warned by several other Christian groups that we would be rejected immediately if it was discovered that we were Christians. Not only did we tell the officials that we were Christians, we told them that we were going to be very open about our faith while in their country.

Amazingly, despite what we had been told to the contrary, the fact that we were Christians didn't seem to be a problem at all.

I was intrigued with this response, so after the visit of the *Anastasis* to one of these countries, I went to a top government leader and asked why we had not been stopped from openly preaching the Gospel while in her country.

She said to me, "You don't understand the weight on us as leaders today. We do not have an infrastructure, we don't have a foreign exchange. We are in such need. You provided a place for 2,000 women to give birth on the outskirts of our city. You could be Marxist—we don't care."

I got her point. The needs of her nation were so great that she didn't care what religion we were, so long as we offered solutions.

As we have already seen, down through Church history acts of mercy and kindness have opened up nations and continents to the Gospel. And the same is true today.

Mercy can open nations resistant to other forms of evangelism. Mercy is the Gospel in action for all to see. And as the saying goes, actions speak louder than words. Where words can antagonize, mercy offers the incontrovertible truth that God is love, that He cares about people, that He understands them, and that He bears with them in their need. And as individuals are touched by this truth, nations are changed and doors are opened for the Christian faith to come in.

The challenge for us in the Church today is to once again embrace and practice mercy.

In the earlier quote from *The Spreading Flame*, Professor F. F. Bruce told of the third-century outbreak of plague in Alexandria and how Christians responded to it. He pointed out that because the compassionate response of Christians was so completely opposite to that of the pagan dwellers of the city, the spread of the Gospel in that region was greatly advanced.

Today we don't face the plague, but we do have an epidemic ravaging sections of our population—AIDS. Imagine if Christians began ministering to those dying of this disease, not even caring if they caught the disease in the process, as those Christians in Alexandria hadn't cared. The impact of their actions would resound far and wide. People would see the living Christ incarnate in each person who reached out with a hand of mercy and compassion to soothe the pain of tortured, dying people. Echoes of mercy would reverberate throughout the land.

"Freely you have received, freely give." That is the challenge Jesus places before each one of His disciples. We have freely received from Him; the next move is ours.

> Do not be surprised, my brothers, if the world hates you. We know that we have passed from death to life, because we love our brothers....This is how we know what love is: Jesus Christ laid down his life for us. And we ought to lay down our lives for our brothers. If anyone has material possessions and sees his brother in need but has no pity on him, how can the love of God be in him? Dear children, let us not love with words or tongue but with actions and in truth.
>
> I John 3:13-18

Chapter Three

Hindrances to Mercy

*Kindness has converted more sinners than zeal,
eloquence, and learning.* —*Frederick Faber*

WHEN I WAS GROWING UP, "aids" re-
ferred to the colorful charts and other paraphernalia
teachers used to help us learn better. But not any more.
AIDS now refers to the disease that has reached epidemic level throughout our world. It was only in 1981
that the disease was first detected in North America
among homosexual men. Today, the World Health Organization estimates that between 30 to 40 million people will be infected worldwide by the year 2000.

For the Church, how to respond to the AIDS
epidemic is a thorny issue. However, the debate over the
Church's response has brought into sharp focus some
long-held misconceptions about mercy—misconceptions that hinder the flow of mercy to the needy.

Many in the Church, understanding that AIDS was

first discovered to be transmitted mainly through intravenous drug use and homosexual activity, came to the quick conclusion that it was God's judgment upon those involved in such lifestyles.

Their reasoning was simple. Christians recognize from Scripture that homosexuality is immoral and is therefore sin. Thus, the AIDS epidemic represented God's judgment upon homosexuals, and the Church had better not step in and interfere with God's judgment. AIDS sufferers were deemed not to be worthy of mercy because their sin was so great that they had fallen under God's wrath.

These Christians had done the obvious; they had put two and two together. Unfortunately, they came up with five!

Their reasoning was based upon the Pharisaic notion that there are degrees of sin. And those who follow this reasoning become obsessed with categorizing it. People are then ranked by how bad of a sinner they are perceived to be. But before these Christians know it, their human nature takes over and they find themselves judging harshly those they perceive as worse sinners than themselves—such as those with AIDS.

Aware of this tendency, the apostle Paul warned,

> Therefore judge nothing before the appointed time; wait till the Lord comes. He will bring to light what is hidden in darkness and will expose the motives of men's hearts. At that time each will receive his praise from God.
>
> I Corinthians 4:5

Unwittingly, many of us have not heeded Paul's warning and have raced ahead, judging others, especially those we think are suffering because of their sin. Such judgment, however, becomes a roadblock to the flow of

God's mercy to those who desperately need it.

A subtle variation on this theme is the kind of judgment that occurs when we tell ourselves that a person could have avoided their present circumstances by making smarter choices.

This line of reasoning is becoming more pervasive as technology and research link more and more illnesses directly to lifestyle choices. We now know that smoking causes lung cancer; being overweight contributes to heart disease, high blood pressure, and diabetes; and failing to use sunscreen can result in skin cancer.

Unfortunately, instead of using such information in a positive way to influence and change people's life-styles, all too often we use it to form the basis of our judgments about them. "He deserves heart disease. Look at the way he's abused his body. He's brought it on himself."

With these kinds of cursory judgments, we can quickly absolve ourselves from any obligation to respond in love or mercy. But none of us should presume to have the wisdom to know whose sins are minimal enough to warrant our mercy, and whose sins are so bad that this person would never be worthy of mercy.

Even if our shallow judgments were justified, they are beside the point. Mercy, in the biblical context, is not about right or wrong. Neither is it about analyzing the roots of a person's problem to see if the person deserves our help. Mercy should not be dispensed according to the origin of the need.

Instead, mercy has to do with not prejudging a person, but choosing instead to reach out and help them in Jesus' name. Mercy is about taking our eyes off the person's past, and concentrating on his present and future situation.

Such action is clearly seen in the life of Jesus. During Jesus' time on earth there was a disease equally as devastating as AIDS is to people today. The disease was leprosy, and people who caught it were said to be unclean.

Lepers were the scourge of ancient society; they were outcasts. When out in public, they had to ring a bell and shout, "Unclean, unclean," to warn people they were approaching. Healthy people shunned lepers, refusing to touch them or have anything to do with them. And so, too, did the religious leaders of the day. But not Jesus. He reached out to lepers. He touched them, talked to them, and healed them. He responded to them with compassion, not in judgment or fear of the disease (Luke 5:12-16; 17:11-19).

One day a group of Pharisees brought to Jesus a woman they had caught committing adultery. There was no doubt about her guilt. She had sinned, and the penalty for her sin was death.

The Pharisees, eager to trick Jesus, challenged Him to pronounce the ultimate judgment upon her. But Jesus merely leaned forward, wrote a few things in the sand, and said, "If any one of you is without sin, let him be the first to throw a stone at her" (John 8:7).

One by one, the men who had brought the woman to Jesus turned and walked away. They had come to outwit Jesus; instead, He had brought them face to face with the darkness of their own souls. They came to judge; He pointed out to them their self-righteous position and their own need of judgment.

If God were truly to deal with people according to the wrongs they had done, who of us could stand? As the writer of Ecclesiastes said, "There is not a righteous man on earth who does what is right and never sins"

(Ecclesiastes 7:20).

Paul echoed this thought in his letter to the Romans.

> What shall we conclude then? Are we any better? Not at all! We have already made the charge that Jews and Gentiles alike are all under sin. As it is written: "There is no one righteous, not even one; there is no one who understands, no one who seeks God."
>
> Romans 3:9-11

This casts things in a different light. We are sinners saved by the grace and mercy of our Lord Jesus Christ. And as sinners saved by grace, we are not instructed to judge others, but to be dispensers of Christ's mercy and compassion. If we insist upon judging and categorizing people as our means of determining whether or not they are worthy of our assistance, then the Bible is very specific: The measuring rod we use on other people will be used on us. And as we have already seen, we are all guilty; we have all sinned.

In his book, *I Was Just Wondering*, Philip Yancey makes the following observation.

> In our churches, why not spend more time discussing the implications of Jesus' parable of the righteous man and the tax collector? One man thanked God for his blessings, that he was not a robber, evildoer, adulterer, or tax collector. He fasted twice a week and tithed his income. The other had an indefensible morality, not much in the way of a résumé, and a thoroughly inadequate theology. One prayed eloquently; the other said seven simple words, "God, have mercy on me, a sinner." Yet which

one went home justified? [6]

God is a God of mercy. That is His first response toward people, even people worthy of His judgment. And if that is the way God responds to people, can we, His followers, do anything less?

It was said of Jesus: "A bruised reed he will not break, and a smoldering wick he will not snuff out" (Matthew 12:20).

May the same thing be said of us, too. Wherever there is a need for mercy, we should be the ones to extend it. And our eyes should be fixed firmly on the person's future redemption, not on their past failures.

Judging others rather than being merciful to them is one hindrance to the flow of God's mercy in our world. But there are other hindrances that we must be aware of.

☙Lack of Empathy☚

It's not so uncommon these days to hear this sentiment: "People need to start helping themselves first. After all, God helps those who help themselves."

Unfortunately, those who echo such a sentiment make a big mistake. They suppose that everyone has the same capacity to endure adversity as they do. In fact, none of us can ever be sure how we would respond if we found ourselves in a certain situation. Sometimes people face things when they're emotionally or physically drained, and they simply need someone to help them.

Annette found this to be true. She had always been a very capable person, successfully juggling a family, a career, and various church obligations. Then Annette's mother became critically ill with cancer, and Annette flew across the country to be with her, and to support her father.

The weeks dragged by, and Annette's mother hovered between life and death. After five weeks of uncertainty, Annette was emotionally exhausted. Her family was counting on her to hold things together, and that, as well as trying to cope with the sadness she felt over the imminent death of her mother, overwhelmed her.

Soon Annette found herself unable to do anything but the smallest of tasks. The housework, normally something she coped with easily, began to pile up. She hardly had the energy to help her father pay his monthly bills, and she was very grateful when someone offered to do the grocery shopping for her—she didn't think she could face all the decisions associated with it. Being unable to cope in a situation, and being dependent upon others for help, was a new experience for Annette.

Finally, after her mother's funeral, Annette returned home to Seattle where she learned that an acquaintance from her church was also dying of cancer.

Joe, always an active person, was in his late thirties. His cancer was well advanced, he was in great pain, and his doctor had given him only a few weeks to live. Joe would be leaving behind his wife, Marcy, and four small children.

Spurred on by her own experience of how emotionally and physically draining it was to be around a dying person for any length of time, Annette decided to help.

She developed a roster of people to contact about helping Marcy with the housework and taking care of the children a couple afternoons a week. She added the members of Marcy and Joe's prayer group, as well as some of their other church friends, and began calling them up.

After an hour on the telephone, Annette collapsed in tears. She didn't want to hear any more excuses. One person told her, "Marcy has more time than me. She doesn't have a job or anything. If she needs help, then so do I."

Another friend told her, "I don't see what the big deal is. Joe has a nurse with him, and Marcy has her house pretty organized. I wish my life were that organized."

While Annette was distressed at the responses of these people, she recognized that before she'd had to cope with her mother's slow death, she would have had similar excuses.

Finally, however, Annette did get a small group of people to help Marcy during the period of Joe's slow death. Later, after Joe's funeral, Marcy thanked Annette, saying, "You gave me the thing that was the most precious in the world to me: time free from other concerns to spend a few more hours with Joe. I'll never have that chance again."

How easy it is to look at a situation logically. We all do it at some time or another. We say to ourselves, "Come on, she should be able to cope with that situation on her own. If it were me I'd handle it without help," or some other such sentiment. And indeed, there may be some validity to what we say. Unfortunately, valid or not, such judgments impede the flow of mercy.

"There but for the grace of God go I," is an old saying we're all familiar with. But sometimes it is *too* familiar, and we miss the full importance of its meaning. It defines the attitude we should have when encountering people in crisis. "There but for the grace of God go we." Given a different set of circumstances, that person panhandling on the street, that impoverished refugee, or that person dying of AIDS, could have been us.

Through personal experience, Annette discovered that it is more redemptive to empathize with a person in need than it is to criticize them, no matter how valid our criticism may be. If we must err, then it had best be on the side of mercy and compassion. Anything else is a hindrance to the free expression of God's love and mercy for people.

ᴥWhat about the Needy People in My Home Town?ᴥ

In my capacity as the Director of Mercy Ships, I find myself often speaking on behalf of needy people in far-off places around the world. Sometimes after I've spoken in a church or some other gathering, a person will come up to me and ask, "Why should we give to help people on the other side of the world when there are so many people right here in this city with needs?"

The question I would always like to ask them, but don't, is, "And how much do you give to help the poor and needy locally?" I suspect that in many cases their answer would be, "Very little."

Most often the question is asked in an attempt to deflect the focus from the real issue onto a side issue, thus making the asker feel justified in his position— which often is doing nothing.

Certainly as Christians we have an obligation to minister to the poor and needy around us. But our obligation to extend mercy also goes beyond our home town and our country.

God isn't regional in His thinking. He sees things on a global scale. He sees people in need in Central Africa, and He sees Christians with the means to meet those needs in the United States, Australia, New Zealand, or Europe, and He sends them to meet the need.

The parable of the Good Samaritan clearly points out that our neighbor is not necessarily the person who lives next door to us, but anyone who is in need, regardless of where he resides on planet Earth. Jesus told His followers to go into all the world.

As Christians, we need to beware of becoming so engrossed in our own culture and the needs of our own people that we forget the needs of people in other parts of the world. Some areas of the world bear a disproportionate load of pain and suffering. Sometimes there are obvious reasons why this is so, such as war and other civil disturbances, and other times there are not.

Whatever the cause, as followers of Christ, the words of the Prophet should ring in our ears: "He has showed you, O man, what is good. And what does the Lord require of you? To act justly and to love mercy and to walk humbly with your God" (Micah 6:8).

Acting justly and dispensing mercy to people does not mean we will necessarily alleviate all the suffering in a particular geographic location. However, each person is an individual and worthy of another person's individual attention. And that is what we are asked to do in Jesus' name—minister to other individuals.

Yes, there are many needy people in our cities. And the good news is, we can do something about them.

We can give of ourselves to help meet their needs. Perhaps we could get involved in helping at a center for the homeless once a week.

Maybe the need is even closer to home. There could be elderly people living in our neighborhood who are unable to take adequate care of themselves. Perhaps we could help them take care of their house, or we could take them to the supermarket to buy groceries. We could even fix dinner for them once or twice a week.

Maybe they are lonely and need someone to talk to. Whatever the needs in our local community, we can help by giving of ourselves selflessly and unto the Lord.

౭Isn't a Person's Spiritual State More Important?౭

Another hindrance to the flow of mercy is summed up in this question: "Isn't improving the person's spiritual condition more important than worrying about his physical condition? After all, it's better to be starving and get to heaven than it is to have a full belly and wind up in hell!"

Again, there is an element of truth in this question. Certainly a person's spiritual state is important, and it cannot be overlooked for one minute. However, as one group of young people on an evangelism team from Youth With A Mission found out, sometimes you have to deal with a person's physical condition before you can deal with his spiritual situation. The YWAM team was evangelizing in East Africa when they came upon a starving man. They began to share the Gospel message with the man, but he just looked at them and said, "I can't hear you; I'm too hungry." The man had an obvious physical need, and no matter how good the good news they had to share with him was, it didn't meet his most obvious need. Their words didn't take away the gnawing hunger in the man's stomach.

Amy Carmichael was one of the great missionaries of the early twentieth century. For fifty-five years she labored for the Lord in India rescuing girls from a life as Hindu temple prostitutes. She ministered to the girls she rescued in a practical way, concentrating on meeting their physical needs, educating them, and developing their character. But she drew criticism from some of her fellow missionaries in India who thought her approach was too practical and not evangelistic enough. To her detractors, Amy responded: "One cannot save and then pitchfork souls into heaven.... Souls are more or less securely fastened to bodies...as you cannot get the souls out and deal with them separately, you have to take them both together." [7]

Amy Carmichael knew full well that mercy has ramifications that go far beyond the moment. Mercy, given in Jesus' name, is like a lens that focuses the light of eternity on a person's need. Mercy opens the shutters of their heart and lets God's love shine in. Long after we have forgotten performing the act of mercy, the person who received it has not. It is a memory the Holy Spirit can use to draw the person gently closer to the Lord.

Do Something

We must be wary of those things that would hinder us from being God's bearers of mercy. Certainly our world seems overwhelmed with needy people in desperate situations, but we must not let the magnitude of the problem cause us to hide behind excuses and to do nothing. God has not asked us to go into all the world and solve its problems. Our world rests in the hands of God. He is the one who will ultimately deal with the world and all its problems. He has a plan.

But in the meantime, He has asked us to go into all the world and be vessels to deliver His compassion, mercy, and salvation to all people. It is a job too big for one person, one ship-full of people, one ministry, or even one church or denomination. It is a job all Christians are called to partake in.

For some it may take them to the other side of the world; for others it may take them to the other side of their city or their street. We may not know where the need for mercy takes us, or who it will bring us in contact

with, but we do know that it should take us somewhere
and bring us in contact with someone—someone who
needs the touch of God's mercy in his life.

Chapter Four

One to One

PERHAPS, LIKE ME, after a day at work you've sunk into a comfortable recliner, flicked the button on the remote control, and settled in to watch the news. The larger-than-life face of Dan Rather or Peter Jennings fills the screen as he introduces the events of the day.

Then, in the flash of a second, the camera cuts away and new images burst into view—disturbing images, at times gruesome and grotesque.

Images of war: of rocketfire and explosions, of wounded soldiers and maimed civilians. Images of disaster: of families, their ashen faces staring blankly at all that remains of their homes. Images of famine: of fragile, emaciated, living skeletons, the hopelessness of their situation bored into the camera lens in the stare from their glazed eyes. Images of poverty: of filthy children begging on street corners, of homeless men and women huddled over steam vents as a biting wind stings their faces.

Each image carries with it the physical, emotional, and spiritual pain of people caught in the grasp of desperate situations. They are emotionally charged images, images that have the power to bring us to tears. But often those tears aren't forthcoming.

Why?

We are so overwhelmed by the images of people suffering around the world that we have become numb to their plight. We can watch their desperate situation on television, but somehow our minds have become adept at filtering out the emotional charge that comes with the images. So we can watch, but most often we're not really moved in our hearts.

In his book, *A Cry in the Wilderness*, Keith Green makes note of this situation and comments:

> What's the limit of your concern? In the evening we love to sit in our air-conditioned living rooms and watch TV. There on the news we see faces of dying, starving, helpless people. We see people afflicted by war, famine, disease, and other natural disasters. These people aren't being laid at our gate—they're being laid in our living rooms. They look us straight in the eye as we kick back on our cushioned recliners. "Could you bring me some more gravy, dear? My goodness, look at these starving people! Would you mind changing the channel? This is upsetting my dinner."
>
> Are we going to leave the homeless and starving lying helpless on our living room rug?[8]

Keith always had a knack for being blunt, but he makes a good point. The media has changed the way we see and relate to the world. It was not until the end of World War II that the full truth about the genocide of Jewish people in Europe became widely known to the rest of the world. But now, courtesy of the television networks, people not only hear about genocide occurring in Rwanda, they see it first-hand. They see innocent women and children being hacked to death by machete-wielding men, for no other reason than belonging to the wrong tribe. They see thousands of people fleeing their homeland in terror. They see endless streams of dead bodies being washed down muddy rivers. And it isn't old news; it is beamed by satellite from Rwanda to their living rooms.

Another change is in the way we observe the world. Technology, as Keith Green noted, has allowed the suffering and needs of people to be instantaneously beamed into our homes. They are being laid in our living rooms. And as Keith poignantly asked: "Are we going to leave them lying helpless on our living room rug?"

For many of us, sadly, that is where they stay. We've build mechanisms that keep them at arm's length. Perhaps the mechanism we use most is that of stereotyping people into groups.

How does this mechanism work?

Imagine that another typhoon has slammed into Bangladesh, causing widespread destruction and loss of life. On the evening news we see images of people wandering dazed among the devastation. Houses are torn apart, trees broken off, and there is widespread flooding. Among the devastation are many dead bodies. When confronted with these images, many of us sigh and say to ourselves, "Not again! When are these people going to wake up and realize that it's just asking for trouble living on such flat land? Why doesn't the government there build some big dikes or something?"

With that, many of us summarily dismiss what we have just seen. But in making our judgment, we have lumped together the people of Bangladesh and stereotyped them. They have become to us a group of people who daily court disaster because of where they choose to live. But the fact of the matter is that Bangladesh is one of the poorest and most densely populated nations in the world, not to mention the fact that almost the entire country consists of low-lying land. Even if they wanted to move to higher ground, there is none to be found.

So we stereotype people into groups. But too often our stereotyping is based on wrong and inaccurate information. The point of the stereotyping is usually to make us feel smug or superior at the expense of those we are stereotyping.

Organizations that attempt to spread hatred and fear of those who are different are adept at grouping and stereotyping people. They try to get us to look at the group they have targeted as objects of hatred as a whole, as a mass of people bound together by their race, creed, ethnic origin, and any other criterion they choose. Everyone within the group is the same. Thus we can heap our scorn or hatred upon the group.

Those who foster stereotypes would never want us to look at a group of people and see them as individuals—people like you and me—who have feelings, people who can hurt, people who have aspirations and dreams. When we begin to see people that way, we react differently toward them. We begin to empathize with them and feel compassion for them, rather than heaping our scorn and hatred upon them.

Individuals are the building blocks of societies. Groups of people consist of individuals—individuals like us. Thus when we are confronted with a situation, be it via the media or firsthand, we need to see it in terms of its impact on individuals.

Perhaps some things could be done to lessen the devastating impact of typhoons in Bangladesh. Perhaps some things will be done in the future, but right now, individual lives are devastated every time a typhoon slams into that country. Certainly the nation as a whole suffers disruption, but the real suffering occurs at the level of the individuals making up the country. Those dead bodies were people that others loved and cherished. They were husbands, wives, parents, children, brothers, sisters, uncles, aunts, and friends to others—others who each must suffer the loss of the person, and feel the pain of it in their hearts.

Those dazed people staring at piles of rubble are looking at their dreams in ruins. Often they are so overwhelmed by what has happened that they don't know what to do next or how to go on with their lives. Each one is a hurting individual.

It is such a basic fact, but one we can so easily lose sight of. Calamities happen to individuals. They are the ones who must bear its pain and its marks in their lives.

Susan discovered this firsthand. She was a secretary from the United States who joined a Mercy Ships short-term relief team to northern Iraq assisting Kurdish refugees. There were such diverse needs that needed to be addressed in the lives of the Kurds that at times Susan and her teammates felt overwhelmed. They prayed for children, assisted at the first-aid center, and picked up bags of disease-ridden garbage.

When Susan left the refugee camp ten days later, she reflected on her time: "I began to see the Kurds as individuals. They die one by one and they can be helped one by one. For those we helped, our being here was priceless."

Sometimes, though, while we may be aware of people as individuals, we tend to think of them as ignorant, sometimes even less than human. This is especially true for those of us who have grown up in western culture. Subtly we have come to think of ourselves as more advanced than other cultures. We have an arrogance that causes us to view different cultures with suspicion, and sometimes even contempt.

Often we are not aware of such feelings until we're confronted with a situation that brings them to the forefront. That's how it was for Christie, a freshly trained nurse eager to put her newly acquired skills to work in the Philippines.

Christie's first assignment was in a small medical clinic in a squatter community in Manila. One morning, not too long after Christie had arrived, a teenager and an older woman came to the clinic carrying a shoebox-sized bundle wrapped in a filthy towel. Christie watched as they unwrapped the towel to reveal a tiny, emaciated baby girl.

Christie could see that the child was closer to death than to life. She sent her assistant to hail a taxi while she hooked up an I.V. As they rode to the hospital, the grandmother wept silently while the mother, riding in the front seat, reached back anxiously to hold the little girl's hand.

As the taxi wound its way through the maze of narrow streets, the grandmother explained tearfully how they had tried to help the little girl. She was four days old, and because she was obviously premature they had treated her with the best medicine they knew—an exclusive diet of ground snake's liver.

Christie was appalled. How could they feed a tiny baby ground snake's liver? It was going to be a miracle if the small child made it to the hospital alive.

Thankfully, the baby did make it, and with intensive care from Christie, grew strong and healthy.

But the first few weeks of nursing the baby back to health were not easy. Christie found it difficult to relate to the child's mother and grandmother—she held them responsible for the baby's critical condition.

But as Christie continued to watch the women interact with the child, her heart began to soften. They were not a pair of unfeeling adults after all. They really cared about the child. When they had fed snake's liver to the baby, they had been doing all they knew to do.

Christie also learned that just getting the snake's liver had been an ordeal for the grandmother. Each day she'd had to make a twenty-mile jeepney trip into the foothills outside Manila to the village where her brothers lived. She had enlisted their help to catch snakes and extract their livers.

In her first newsletter home Christie wrote:

The thing that we in the West call common sense is not always so common here. I realize now that common sense is something we learn as a result of hearing the same advice from so many quarters such as parents, teachers, the media, books, and we begin to think it's something we're born with.

But it's not; it's something we learned. Here I've seen parents who love their children as much as any westerner loves theirs, do the most bizarre things to help them. I treated a little girl with impetigo. Her father, hoping to seal the wound so it would heal, had painted her head with nail polish. In another instance, an aunt had treated her three-year-old nephew's severe burns with toothpaste. Her reasoning? She knew that some kind of paste was needed to heal burns, and all she could afford was toothpaste.

In the two months I've been here, I have learned one thing: these parents, despite how uncommon their common sense may seem, love their children. Some of them have to watch one child after another die, and often they don't have the luxury of time to mourn; they must get up and keep going. As Westerners it's easy for us to think, "They have no feelings." But from my experience, that is simply not the truth.

Christie was able to articulate what each missionary finds to be true. We are all human beings; when our loved ones are sick or dying, we desperately look for ways that they might be healed.

Each of us needs to ask God to give us the heart and the humility to value people as individuals, not as the stereotypes we may have been influenced into developing about them. A crowd of people begging for food is made up of individual mothers and fathers begging for enough food to silence the cries of their starving children. The tragedy of the way we look at suffering today is that we seldom see it for what it is—suffering individuals, often suffering through situations beyond their control.

☙Meeting the Need☞

It was the late 1940s, and Bob Pierce already had a successful ministry. He served as the Vice-President-at-Large of Youth for Christ, and in that capacity he was sent on a ministry trip to China. He traveled up to the Tibetan border, where he stopped to tour an orphanage.

On the steps of the orphanage lay a little girl, pitifully thin, and unable to muster enough strength to move out of Bob Pierce's way as he stepped over her. When Bob was finally met by one of the orphanage workers, he confronted her as to why a little girl in such obvious need was being ignored. "Why isn't something being done?" he demanded.

Overwrought with caring for four times the number of children the orphanage was built to handle, the worker swooped down and picked up the girl. She then turned to Bob Pierce and thrust the small child into his arms. Looking him straight in the eyes she retorted, "What are *you* going to do about it?"

Bob Pierce never forgot that question. It challenged him. How could he stand in judgment of those who were not doing what he himself was unwilling to do? He decided he had to act, so upon his return to the United States he founded World Vision. For more than forty years the organization he founded has been responsible for providing funds and workers for hundreds of orphanages, homes, clinics, and hospitals around the world.

As we are all well aware, human suffering and need around the world is as great today as it was when Bob Pierce founded World Vision. So the question the orphanage worker asked him needs to be asked of each one of us: Faced with the graphic images of suffering and need that the media sets before us daily, what are *you* going to do about it?

It is a question that demands an answer. Bob Pierce started a ministry, but not all of us are called to do that, and not all of us have the resources or the abilities to do so. But each of us can do something, so what are we going to do? Are we going to do something, or are we going to do nothing?

Many of us would prefer that the question were directed to our church or to a ministry. It would be much easier, then, to ride along with the flow. But God knows our human nature. He knows that people who go with the flow usually end up drifting along, doing as little as possible. So He directs the question to us individually, and we have to make the choice. And not only that, we have to take the responsibility for our choice.

One day, Jesus told His disciples a story which illustrated the importance of making the right choice in answer to the question. He told of a certain rich man who was having a great time here on earth. This man had the finest clothes, the biggest house, and the best wine. He wanted for nothing.

But right outside this man's house was another man, a poor and decrepit beggar named Lazarus. The rich man totally ignored Lazarus and his need. Time passed and eventually both men died. What a role reversal awaited them! Lazarus went straight to be in God's presence, while the rich man went to Hades.

When the rich man looked across the chasm between the two of them, he saw Abraham with Lazarus. So he yelled across, "Father Abraham, have pity on me and send Lazarus to dip the tip of his finger in water and cool my tongue, because I am in agony in this fire."

But Abraham said to him, "Son, remember that in

your lifetime you received your good things, while Lazarus received bad things, but now he is comforted here, and you are in agony" (Luke 16:19-31).

Keith Green made these observation about this story:

> Sometimes I deceive myself into thinking I'm better than the rich man. I think, "If someone were left outside my door, of course I'd take care of his needs." Then how is it that people are starving a few thousand miles away from where I live, and I think I can ignore them?[9]

We are called by God to be dispensers of His mercy, not monitors of the world's suffering. Unfortunately many in the Church find it more comfortable to sit and wait for others—the government, the Church, the Red Cross, the United Nations, ministries—to step in and do something about solving the problem of suffering in the world.

But God calls us as individuals to minister to other individuals. That is the story of the incarnation. Jesus came as a man and ministered to other men. He never held appeals for people to come forward to be ministered to as a group. No, Jesus went to individuals, and individuals were drawn to Him, and He ministered the mercy and compassion of God to them one by one. Now He calls us to follow in His footsteps. What are we going to do? Follow His example, or turn our backs on the suffering and needy people of our world?

"Do to others what you would have them do to you," Jesus said, summing up the law of the prophets (Matthew 7:12). They are wise words to contemplate in relation to how we will respond to the suffering of others. If the tables were turned, and we were the ones suffering, how would we want people to respond to us? Think about it.

Chapter Five

❦

Partnership with God

❦

*Christ cannot live his life today in this world without
our mouth, without our eyes, without our going and
coming, without our heart. When we love,
it is Christ loving through us. This is
Christianity.* —Leon Joseph Suenens

AS A CHILD attending Sunday school, I
was fascinated by the great stories from the Bible. Of
course, I didn't fully understand their meaning. I remember listening with great interest to the story of one
boy who gave his lunch, which Jesus, in turn, used to
feed five thousand people. Not only did He feed them,
but there were leftovers, as well! I put myself in the place
of that boy. I imagined what it would be like to have my
peanut butter and jelly sandwich and my apple become
enough to feed my whole school!

But as I grew up I began to ask myself, "What was
the point? The Lord could have easily produced enough

food to feed several thousand people from absolutely nothing. So why did He need that little boy's lunch?"

And the feeding of the five thousand isn't the only story like that in the Bible. God often seems to use the small, and sometimes insignificant, actions of men to accomplish something big. The children of Israel, for example, had to march around Jericho once each day for six days, and on the seventh day they marched around it seven times and gave a trumpet blast and shouted. When they did so, the walls of Jericho came tumbling down. God delivered the city into their hands (Joshua 6:1-21).

Then there was Moses. God told Moses to raise his staff over the Red Sea. And when he did that, God parted the sea so the children of Israel could escape from the Egyptians (Exodus 14:15-22).

God was the one who parted the Red Sea. He was the one who caused the walls of Jericho to come tumbling down. So why did He need Moses to raise his staff over the sea, or the Israelites to march around Jericho? Why does God choose to work through men and women? Why does He seek their cooperation and their obedience when He is all-powerful and able to accomplish the task without them?

I don't know the full answer to these questions, but one thing is certain: God wants to establish a partnership with men and women to accomplish His will on earth. No matter how uneven the match-up may seem, He wants us to be involved in fulfilling His plans.

God especially wants this partnership to operate in showing His mercy to mankind in tangible ways. The more we come to know Him, and the more we fine-tune our hearts to His concerns for people—especially needy people—the more dynamic and rewarding our partnership with Him becomes.

As I have become involved in extending mercy to others, I am often struck by the way my actions conform to God's orchestrated plans. He wants to extend mercy, and many times He sets things up in such a way that it is extended through me in His name. Over and over we have also seen this to be true in Mercy Ships. We think we have a great plan to do something, only to find that the plan was conceived first in the heart of God, and we are the instruments He is using to carry out His plan.

God is love, and He is mercy. When we dispense mercy, we align ourselves with His heart for the world. It is not until much later that we see the full impact of our small offering of mercy when directed by God. Indeed, I am often humbled by the way God takes our small effort in mercy and surrounds it with a context far more meaningful than anything we could have imagined.

Aminata Sesay is a case in point. Aminata sold cloth in the market in Freetown, Sierra Leone. In a land where the average wage is $27 a month, business was prospering for the hard-working and ambitious nineteen year old. Her future seemed as bright as the colorful printed fabrics she sold.

Aminata had no inkling, though, that the tiny lump she felt one day next to a tooth would alter her future. Initially the lump grew slowly, but then it abruptly ballooned in size. Soon Aminata's friends began to find reasons to avoid her; they were frightened of the power that could cause such a transformation. They suspected the tumor was some kind of omen sent by the gods.

The tumor grew, engulfing her jaw and hanging like a swollen melon on the side of her face. And as it grew, Aminata's business shriveled. Customers found other sources for their fabric. No one wanted to risk purchasing cursed merchandise from such a tormented woman.

Slowly those who had previously ignored Aminata's condition began to taunt her, calling her the "Witch of Freetown." She felt too vulnerable to show her face in public. She kept away from people, and to keep from starving, peeled oranges and sold them at the side of the road, where she kept her head bowed and the left side of her face turned away from prying eyes.

During this time, Aminata sought out local doctors. Each told her the same thing: They could remove the tumor, but unfortunately they would have to remove her jawbone along with it. She would be medically stable, but the operation would leave her even more disfigured— with no hope of improvement. Aminata was faced with a dilemma. The cure would be worse than the ailment, at least in cultural terms. So as she sat among the oranges, watching feet hurry by, willing people to stop and buy from her, there seemed no hope left.

But Aminata was a very determined young lady. The determination that had driven her on to establish her own business at age nineteen began to rise within her. Even though it seemed hopeless, there was an answer and she was going to find it, regardless of how long it took. Her Muslim faith offered little hope, so she began attending a Christian church. The contrast was startling to her. As she later reflected, "I felt peace inside, happy because I believed in Jesus. Things got difficult for me. My friends laughed and cursed me. They called me a witch, but I would pray, 'God help me. Protect me. I am Your daughter. I believe You will heal me one day.'"

And so Aminata prayed, believed, and waited. As she waited, the tumor continued growing, but so did her confidence that Jesus would heal her.

While praying one day in 1991, an unusual thought lodged in her mind. "The time is coming. Next year you will be healed." She recognized it as the voice of the Lord speaking to her. Aminata began to cry huge tears of relief; God had heard her prayers. As she drifted off to sleep that night she prayed, "Papa God, I believe You. Send people to me so Your power and blessing will be seen." That night Aminata had a dream. In her dream she saw foreigners come to Freetown, where they operated on her and she was healed. The dream sealed things in Aminata's mind; 1992 was the year she would be healed!

And so it was that in November 1992, Mercy Ships Assistant Nursing Coordinator Debbie Bergey and her team made their way through the crowd waiting to have their medical conditions assessed. Some babies were crying; others were too weak to cry. Old people crippled from arthritis and dietary deficiencies were crowded in with others having various medical problems.

As usual, the team felt overwhelmed with the need. They could stay in Sierra Leone a year or even two years ministering continuously, and still not see an end to the human suffering and sadness. The need was so great and the workers were so few.

Debbie started interviewing the young woman in front of her. The young woman's face was so badly distorted by a huge tumor that it was hard to tell her age. Debbie supposed she might have been pretty once, but it was hard to say.

Drooling continuously, and with a great deal of physical difficulty, the young woman told Debbie her name was Aminata Sesay, and explained some of her case history. A thorough examination ensued, revealing that the tumor had completely eaten into Aminata's left jaw, pushed up the roof of her mouth, and forced her tongue permanently against her cheek, making it difficult for her to speak.

Aminata's condition was exactly the type of condition the *Anastasis* hospital was equipped to deal with. They quickly decided that she would be operated on by the ship's medical team. Aminata had found help at last!

Announcing the decision to Aminata, Debbie had no way of knowing that the good news she shared was a source of double blessing. First, after thirteen long years Aminata would finally be rid of the tumor—and have a new jaw reconstructed in the process. Second, in offering mercy to Aminata, Debbie became one of the team members Aminata had seen in her dream.

The dream had given Aminata the faith to believe for the impossible. Now she knew firsthand that God really cared about her and her situation. Indeed He cared for her so much that He'd orchestrated events to make her healing possible.

Two weeks later, a surgical team on board the M/V *Anastasis* removed the five-inch tumor that had clung fiercely to the side of Aminata's face for 13 years. Then they took bone grafts from two of her ribs and her pelvis to reconstruct a new jaw—the thing her previous offers of medical help had been unable to deliver—and after another two weeks she was released from the hospital.

When Aminata returned to the *Anastasis* for a checkup, she told the staff about her homecoming. "Everyone started jumping up and down when they saw me. I told them, 'You see, I believed Jesus, and now He has healed me! He did what He promised He would do.'"

Today, Aminata Sesay has her beautiful, smiling face back. And that face radiates each time she tells someone, "You see, Jesus told me He would heal me, and He did."

Aminata's story is dramatic, but not that unfamiliar to the staff of Mercy Ships. We continue to hear of similar situations where God has prepared people to receive healing or some other act of mercy before we have even arrived in a country. But Aminata's story reminds us of the unfathomable balance of God and man interacting together to bring faith and healing to others.

From the human side, Aminata received healing by the hands of skilled surgeons and professional medical staff who nursed her back to health. Their dedication and expertise alone were a tremendous gift to a poor person in Sierra Leone.

From the divine side, God went before us. He assured Aminata that He had a plan to heal her, sending a dream to seal His words, and giving her faith to stand firm in the face of the ridicule she received from her Muslim friends.

When the medical staff operated on Aminata, they were the fulfillment of God's promise to her. They were the flesh and blood outworking of the dream. And therein lies the partnership: God, with all the resources of the universe at His disposal, used people to bring His promises to pass.

While Scripture exhorts us to have faith in God, what about the other side of the equation? To establish a partnership with us and use us to bring His mercy to those in desperate need, God must also have faith in us.

Imagine if the crew of the *Anastasis* had decided to take a break instead of going to Sierra Leone, or if our faithful financial partners had not honored their pledges that month. Where would Aminata be? She would have had her dream about being healed, she would have proclaimed her faith in Jesus, but her healing would not have come—at least not through the Mercy Ships crew.

God trusts us to do our part, as He is doing His. In comparison to His part, our part often seems small, but in the outworkings of God's kingdom, it is a vital part.

The ramifications of this human/divine partnership in Aminata's life go far beyond her healing. Her family has seen the power of the living God at work. And in Freetown, Sierra Leone, there is a living, breathing, active witness for the Lord Jesus Christ. In all she does, Aminata wants to bring glory to God—the one person who, when everyone else abandoned her, was faithful to her and answered her cry for help.

But before a person can bring glory to God, he must first experience God's glory and power at work. That was true in Aminata's case, and it was true in the life of the man blind from birth whom Jesus healed:

> As he went along, he saw a man blind from birth. His disciples asked him, "Rabbi, who sinned, this man or his parents, that he was born blind?"
>
> "Neither this man nor his parents sinned," said Jesus, "but this happened so that the work of God might be displayed in his life."
>
> John 9:1-3

Jesus went on to heal the man by spitting on the ground and making mud which He then put on the blind man's eyes and told him to go and wash in the pool of Siloam. When the blind man did so, he could see. The work of God had been displayed in his life. He had experienced firsthand the glory and power of God. As a result, his life was changed forever. He could see for the first time. Friends and family were amazed. Some even thought that it wasn't the blind man at all, but a double. But the man who had been blind testified to what had happened to him. Even when he was dragged before the suspicious and spiteful Pharisees, he held fast to his testimony. He had experienced the touch of God on his life, and nothing would persuade him otherwise.

When Jesus heard of the man's tenacious witness to what had happened to him, He went and found the man. Together they talked until the formerly blind man recognized that Jesus was the Son of Man. I am sure that for the rest of his life, the once-blind man would not stop telling people about what had happened to him, and giving God the glory at every turn.

That is what an act of mercy can do for a person. Through an act of mercy, a person can experience first-hand the power of God at work in his life. And having experienced God at work in his life, he can bring great glory to Him.

Five thousand hungry people experienced the power of God through the partnership of a small boy who handed over his meager lunch and allowed Jesus to multiply it and feed the hungry throng. We, too, are called to become partners with God in order that others might experience His mercy and His power in their lives.

Our partnership with Him is often seen in many small ways. We don't have to have a mercy ship or a big ministry before we can become a partner with God. We may not be a skilled surgeon or a professional health-care worker. Extending mercy goes far beyond simply extending medical aid. We can administer mercy in a million different ways: buying groceries for someone who is poor, taking an unwed mother into our home, helping people rebuild their lives and homes after some natural disaster, or even mowing the lawn for an elderly neighbor. The specific act of mercy is not as important as our availability to be a partner with God.

I read a quote once that has stuck with me: "Between the great things we cannot do and the little things

we will not do, the danger is that we will do nothing"
(H. G. Weaver).

How true that is! We must never forget that we are
God's hands and feet in this world. We are the ones who
are the living, breathing expressions of His love and
concern for mankind. So we must do something. We
must act. We must become His expressions of love and
mercy. The ball is in our court. God wants to be partners
with us in this endeavor. Are we ready to become partners with Him?

Chapter Six

❧❧

Valuing Value

❧❧

CANCRUM ORIS IS A DISEASE that starts as a small ulcer on the gums. The ulcer grows as time goes by, eating away flesh and bone as it does so. And that is how the disease had progressed for N'Balou Cherif. For twenty-three of her twenty-six years, the aftermath of *cancrum oris* had been her unwelcome companion. For N'Balou it had started as a small sore in her mouth which, over the years, had eaten away her right cheek and jawbone, making it very difficult for her to eat, and impossible to talk.

One day someone told N'Balou about a medical team in the far-off port city of Conakry who could help her overcome her disease. With the aid of her half-sister, Djeneba, N'Balou set out from her village in the Mandingo region of Guinea for Conakry in the south. But her long journey was met with disappointment when she arrived in Conakry. The medical team had been attached to the M/V *Anastasis,* and the *Anastasis* was about to return to Europe for restocking. However, one of the crew members assured N'Balou that the ship would return and would be able to help her.

Nonetheless, it was a dejected N'Balou who made the return trip home. Along the way she struggled with her feelings. It had been a foolhardy gesture—N'Balou knew it. After all, she was just a poor woman from a small village in northern Guinea with a debilitating affliction. She had been the object of people's jokes and scorn most of her life, so who did she think she was to go running off after a visiting medical team, thinking they would be interested in her plight? Why would they want to bring a huge ship back from Europe to help the likes of her? The more she thought about it, the more preposterous it sounded. Yet despite her doubts, N'Balou found herself clinging to the promise that the medical team would return.

For the next eight long months she battled doubt and despair as she clung to the promise that the team would return. And then in early November, an official letter arrived for N'Balou. The *Anastasis* was coming back, just as she had been promised! And the medical team wanted to help her. They had scheduled her for surgery on November 27. With a mixture of disbelief and excitement, N'Balou packed a small bag and boarded the bus with Djeneba for the 400-kilometer trip to Freetown, Sierra Leone, where the M/V *Anastasis* was docked.

In Freetown, tears streaming down their faces, the two girls made their way along the dock toward the big white ship that lay peacefully at its mooring. As N'Balou stepped on board, it was almost too much for her to take in. The team had come back for her.

Throughout the next month, Djeneba stayed quietly at her sister's side through three separate operations. She helped N'Balou exercise her atrophied muscles and regain the use of her mouth. She listened to N'Balou's first few words, and fed her the first bites of normal food. And as she watched over the recovery of her sister, Djeneba's dark eyes also paid close attention to the crew and members of the medical team. Nothing escaped her gaze.

Christmas came and went, as did New Year, and finally on January 30, N'Balou was released to go home. The crew gathered to say farewell to N'Balou and her sister after the girls' nine weeks on board. At that farewell Djeneba spoke up on behalf of N'Balou and herself. "We came here and you treated us as if there were no difference in our skin color," she said in a clear and decisive voice. "You could have given us money; we would have spent it. You could have given us clothes; they would have worn out. But you gave my sister much more: You gave her a new face and the ability to open her mouth. You showed us love and respect. You showed us how to be Christians. Now we want to go home and live as Christians, as you have shown us."

To those who had ministered to N'Balou during her time on board, Djeneba's words were profound. Through meeting the physical needs of an African girl they had given her something more than good health— they had bestowed upon her a sense of value. N'Balou, who had known so much ridicule and scorn in her life, had been treated like a human being, a fact that had not gone unnoticed by her sister.

Every human being has this same desire to be valued by others. Each of us desires to be treated with dignity and respect. By performing an act of mercy and kindness for another person, we not only meet the immediate physical need, but we also reach in and touch the deep emotional need to be valued.

Jesus was well aware of this need in His dealings with people. Whether they were young or old, healthy or infirm, loved or despised, He bestowed upon them a sense of value. He showed them respect regardless of their social, ethnic, or economic station in life. And by having value bestowed upon them, people's lives were changed.

Take, for example, Jesus' encounter with Zacchaeus (Luke 19:1-10). It would be fair to say that Zacchaeus was not well-liked by his fellow Jews. To them he was an infidel. He had sold himself out to the Romans for the privilege of collecting taxes, with a little ill-gotten gain on the side. And worse, he flaunted his deceit while hiding behind the power of the Roman legions.

Then one day, Jesus came to town. Zacchaeus was eager to catch a glimpse of this man many were referring to as the Messiah—the one who would deliver Israel from the hands of the Romans.

Unable to secure a better viewing position, the hated Zacchaeus found himself a perch in a nearby sycamore tree. To the tax collector's fascination and amazement, Jesus jostled His way through the crowd until He stood beneath the tree. Jesus and Zacchaeus locked eyes while those in the crowd held their breath and waited for the sharp rebuke Jesus would deliver to this despised and deceitful sell-out. And Zacchaeus held his breath, too.

But to Zacchaeus' relief, and the crowd's consternation, the rebuke was not forthcoming. Instead, Jesus said, "Zacchaeus, come down out of the tree. I want to spend the evening at your house."

Zacchaeus almost fell out of the tree! Why would this holy man want to spend the evening with him?

As the crowd mumbled among themselves, Zacchaeus escorted Jesus to his home.

Safely inside they sat and talked, and it wasn't too long before Zacchaeus proclaimed, "Lord, here and now I give half of my possessions to the poor, and if I have cheated anybody out of anything, I will pay back four times the amount."

These were the words of a changed man!

What had happened?

Everyone, including his Roman overlords, despised Zacchaeus. So when Jesus—the most popular teacher of the time—asked Zacchaeus to spend time with Him, Zacchaeus was deeply touched.

Jesus had treated him with dignity. He had bestowed value upon him, and in the process, Zacchaeus' life had been changed. He wanted to change his ways, and the only way he knew how was by giving away more than he had cheated and extorted from people over the years, just as Jesus had given him more love and respect than he deserved.

What about those who'd been muttering among themselves about Jesus spending time with this notorious infidel and sinner? I'm sure they quickly changed their tune when they heard Zacchaeus' declaration. "Perhaps Jesus knew what He was doing after all. Perhaps He saw some streak of good in Zacchaeus that we couldn't see," they may have said to themselves.

Anyone could have come to town and preached about equality and the value of an individual, and the need to treat people as people, regardless of their race, religion, sex, or social standing. But Jesus was a man of action. He showed people, rather than told them, how they should live their lives. By spending time with Zacchaeus, Jesus had not only bestowed value upon him, but he had also demonstrated to those in the crowd how they should respond, even toward people they despised.

This was a message Jesus reiterated many times during His time on earth through His actions toward prostitutes, publicans, tax collectors, and other sinners. He treated each of them as a special individual—special to Him and special to His Father.

In his book, *52 Ways to Help the Homeless*, Gray Temple, Jr. makes a similar point.

> The trick is to enjoy your new friends. That's love. It restores human community.... Homeless people are accustomed to having people like you stare through them, avoid catching their eyes, and walk on past. They come to know that they are invisible to most of us. If you enjoy the company of homeless persons, you give them the gift of knowing that somebody realizes they exist. That's at least as significant as food and shelter.[10]

Through offering mercy to the individual, we can follow in Jesus' footsteps. Through our actions, we can show people that they are worthy of receiving love, attention, and kindness. And when others receive mercy from us, we open the door for their lives to be changed.

Our compassionate actions can also help others see people through different eyes. Mercy cuts through prejudice and stereotypes, and focuses attention on the obvious need of the individual. And such a change of focus can change the way people relate to each other.

That's how it was with Zacchaeus. The way Zacchaeus cheated and extorted money from his fellow Jews was reprehensible. His actions had caused people to become prejudiced against him. But their prejudice, in turn, blinded them to the fact that inside, Zacchaeus was deeply troubled over his corrupt lifestyle. Jesus, though, saw past the prejudice to Zacchaeus' obvious need, and reached out to him. That simple act of compassion brought Zacchaeus' inner turmoil into sharp focus. And seeing what he saw, he decided to turn his back on his old ways.

Of course, I'm sure that after Zacchaeus had given half of all he had to the poor and returned fourfold to people what he had cheated from them, they viewed him differently. Their prejudice was broken down. Zacchaeus had become a man worthy of their love and respect.

Stan Evans had an experience that also illustrates how an act of mercy can make an invisible person visible again.

It was a late December afternoon when Stan set out from the *Good Samaritan* for a stroll along Presidente Vargas Avenue, in Belem, Brazil. The stores were already closed and the street was almost deserted. As he made his way along the street, Stan came upon a man he presumed to be drunk, sleeping restlessly on the sidewalk.

For some reason Stan decided to take a closer look. The emaciated young man had matted hair and body lice, and even in his sleep he brushed at biting insects. One arm was thinner than the other, and his right foot looked as though it had been carved out of partially burned coal. What remained of the foot was mostly black, dotted with some brown and some ashen-white, flesh. A half-inch thick slice of heel hung off the sole of his foot. Stan recognized the condition immediately as gangrene.

As he stood over the sleeping man, Stan had a decision to make. Should he reach out in mercy or should he walk on? Common sense urged him to move on. After all, Stan spoke no Portuguese, he had no knowledge of the hospital system in Brazil, he had little money, and besides, he didn't even know if the man wanted help!

But as he stood there on the deserted street, he decided to become involved. He returned to the *Good Samaritan* and enlisted the help of a nurse, as well as someone fluent in Portuguese. By the time the three returned, the man had awakened and was sitting up.

They found out his name was Juan Luis. Stan had the interpreter explain that they were going to take him to a hospital. Juan Luis seemed indifferent to his fate. Hospitals cost money, and he had tried to get help before. What good had it done? None. No one wanted to know a street person with gangrene. No one cared.

Despite Juan's pessimism, Stan flagged down a taxi and helped him in. They arrived at the hospital and Juan Luis was taken into a waiting room. Finally he was examined and his condition was deemed to be chronic, which, as Stan was to quickly find out, meant no one was prepared to do anything about it.

So Stan and his friends decided to try another hospital. The response was the same. Juan Luis had a chronic condition and there was nothing they could do. So on they went to yet another hospital.

Juan Luis remained calm throughout the ordeal. He had no expectation of actually receiving help, and so was not disappointed.

At the next hospital they were shown to the office of the hospital director, a pleasant professional woman named Dr. Regina. Stan began to share with her how he felt compelled by God to help Juan Luis. Dr. Regina showed great interest in what Stan had to say. As they talked, her attention began to shift to Juan Luis, and she asked him some penetrating questions as she started filling out the myriad of necessary hospital forms. Finally she made a number of phone calls. Something was happening!

Within the hour, Juan Luis was admitted to the hospital. Doctors gathered to discuss a surgical procedure that might save his leg. Dr. Regina contacted an agency in the city which worked with street people, and after the operation, Juan Luis would be discharged into their care for his convalescence.

Stan waved goodbye as a broadly grinning Juan Luis was wheeled away for a bath and a bed—neither of which he'd seen for a very long time.

Stan's decision to show mercy to Juan Luis had touched Dr. Regina deeply. As he explained to her how important Juan Luis was to God, Dr. Regina began to see Juan through different eyes. He was no longer just one of the many thousands of needy, hopeless, cast-offs who lived on the streets of Belem: he had become a person—a person worthy of her compassion and help.

Dave Anderson left his native Montana to work among the poor of Manila. In a corner of that sweltering, overcrowded city he found squatters who were despised by everyone from government leaders to other squatters. They were the lowest of the low, living in quiet desperation in ramshackle shanties on the city's garbage dump.

These people's lives were harsh and often brutal. Infectious diseases and malnutrition were constant companions. When the people ventured off the dump, they were recognized and unanimously shunned because they smelled of smoky garbage. Most people simply thought of them as beyond help, but not Dave. He established a health-care ministry to meet the needs of these people.

At first Dave seemed to make no headway. The people were suspicious of outsiders. Government leaders tried to discourage the team in their efforts, and those in the community around the dump gossiped among themselves, skeptical of the motives that would bring people halfway around the world to work among these hopeless dump people.

But Dave was a man of immense tenacity and compassion. He kept at his ministry, and things began to happen. Gradually the health of the squatter community began to improve. He began experimenting with ways to provide the people with employment and a way out of the dump. He organized sponsors for the children so they could attend school. Most of the children had been unable to attend school—although it was technically free, the children often didn't have proper clothing, and had no pencils or paper to take with them.

Little by little, the morale of the community began to turn. Despair gave way to hope. People accepted Christ into their lives, and Bible studies began to spring up. People in the dump community began to experience a sense of value. Other people really did care about them! For once, people were treating them like human beings.

Surprisingly to many, the attitude of government and the surrounding community began to change. Indeed, the President of the Philippines lent her support to a project to build a water tower with a distribution system for the dump community. And the Department of Social Welfare and Development found practical ways they could help. They even provided free meals to all those involved in the building of the water system.

Such is the power of mercy. Through getting

involved, Dave Anderson and his team had opened the eyes of government officials and others to see those who lived on the dump differently. These people could no longer pretend to be blind to the desperate plight of those on the dump—they needed to take action. Not only did the perceptions of others change, but those who lived on the dump came to view themselves differently. They began to feel valued; they began to regain a sense of dignity.

Simonne Dyer is a vice-president of Mercy Ships and CEO of our flagship. In 1992, the ship was in Conakry, Guinea, the capital of a Muslim nation in West Africa. As Simonne became acquainted with Muslims in the city and learned more about them, she began to pray. Then one of the crew came to her with a suggestion.

The Muslim month of Ramadan was approaching. During this month the entire Muslim world fasts each day from sunrise to sunset. It is one of their most important religious observances. The crewman suggested that they fast and pray during Ramadan. So began the first Ramadan prayer time aboard ship.

A local mosque in the city began to speak negatively about Mercy Ships. My wife, Deyon, and two of our sons were on board at this time. We heard of this criticism from a Muslim acquaintance of our eldest son, Luke. Naturally I was concerned. I suggested that someone from Mercy Ships meet with the Imam of the mosque or a leader in the nation.

An appointment was made, and within a few days Simonne, a translator, and another French-speaking YWAM leader visited El-hadj Ahmadou Tidjane Traore, Secretary General of the National Islamic League.

At first, as Simonne told Mr. Traore of their work, he seemed stiff and formal. Then Simonne told him her real intent in visiting. She had come out of a deep sense of need to ask him, a Muslim, to forgive the Christians who had inflicted much pain and sorrow on Muslims over the centuries in the name of God.

Mr. Traore was taken aback, but extended forgiveness. Then he asked Simonne to forgive him for failing to come down to the ship and greeting them when they arrived, as was the custom in their country. He expressed his concern over the spiritual lives of his young people, and asked Simonne to keep in touch with the people they had ministered to, as they needed spiritual input. He finished by promising to tell others of their conversation and how she had asked forgiveness.

By coming as servants and humbling themselves, Simonne and the crew of the *Anastasis* had opened a door into a culture that has been closed and hostile to the Gospel of Jesus Christ. They showed Mr. Traore that they valued him and all Muslims.

Jesus did not put people into categories. He respected the beggar as much as the Pharisee, the leper as much as the priest.

More than any other religion, Christianity has enhanced the dignity of each human being, regardless of whether they are male or female, rich or poor, Jew or Gentile. While the world still categorizes people by race, creed, sex, social position, and a million other criteria, the true follower of Christ marches to the beat of a different drum, a color-blind, gender-blind, creed-blind drum. Their drum pulses with the beat that people are valuable—valuable to God and valuable to other people.

No person, regardless of social, ethnic, or economic situation and status, is without value. Instead, they are all objects of God's love, which has been made manifest through the greatest act of mercy the world has ever seen—the incarnation, death, and resurrection of Jesus.

During His time on earth, Jesus showed us that if we are His followers, we must also be channels of God's love and mercy to others. He showed us that through a simple act of mercy we can affirm the value of a person; we can turn him from feeling valueless to feeling valuable. In so doing, we bring the person face to face with the one who imbued him with value in the first place— the Creator of the universe.

Patrick Coker's growing tumor brought him embarrassment and ostracism in his culture. Following surgery he rejoiced saying, "Now I am a new man! I have a new face and I am closer to God."

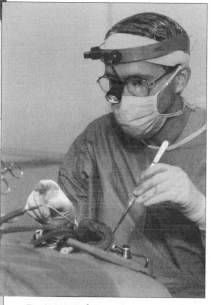

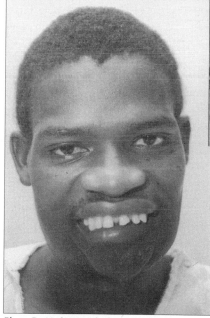

Patients who once covered their heads in shame are now an active part of their societies thanks to surgery on board a mercy ship by Dr. Gary Parker.

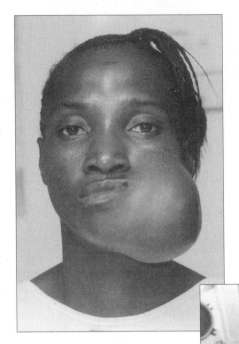

Because of African superstition that tumors are a sign of evil power, Aminata Sesay was called "Witch of Freetown" by her neighbors before her surgery on board a mercy ship.

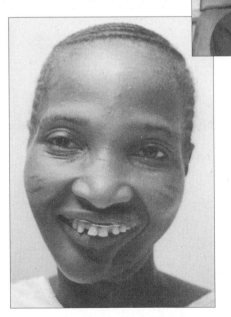

Following her surgery, Aminata quickly gives God the credit for helping her dreams come true through the Mercy Ships crew.

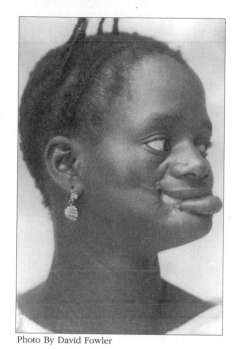

N'Balou Cherif is only one of
the many patients treated by
Mercy Ships for cancrum oris -
known as the "melting disease"
in African culture.

N'Balou can now open her
mouth, thanks to surgery
provided free by Mercy Ships.

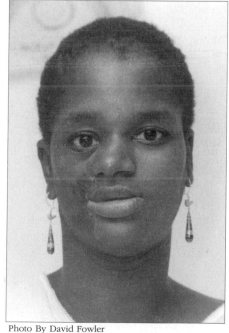

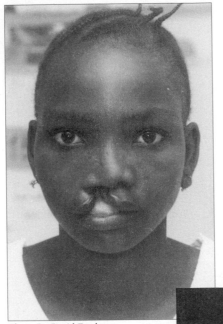

Sixteen-year-old Nana Kamara struggled to speak clearly her whole life. Her cleft-lip impeded both her speech and her ability to eat.

Dr. Gary Parker, Mercy Ships surgeon, spent two hours repairing Nana's cleft lip. A routine surgery for him, it changed the rest of Nana's life.

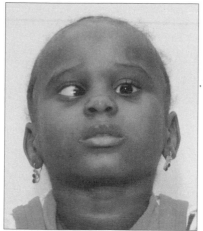

Photo By Chris Bamber

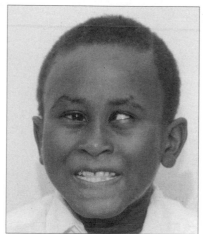

Photo By Chris Bamber

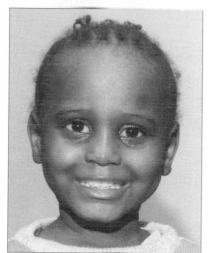

Photo By Chris Bamber

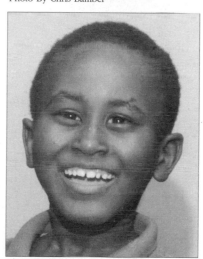

Photo By Chris Bamber

Ami and Sidate Fofana's lives were changed on board a mercy ship. After eight years their mother's prayers were answered, and their crossed eyes were made straight by Mercy Ships ophthalmologist Dr. Bob Dyer.

Anastasis

Length: 522 feet
Breadth: 68 feet
Gross Tonnage: 11,701
Built: 1953 - Trieste, Italy
Registered in Malta
Capacity: 476 berths

Cargo capacity of 3 holds:1,500 tons
Main engines: 2 Fiat diesel
(8,050 hp each)
Draft 23 feet
Surveyed by Lloyds

Caribbean Mercy

Length: 265 feet
Breadth: 40 feet
Gross Tonnage: 2125
Built: 1952 - Aalborg, Denmark
Registered in Panama

Capacity: 160 berths
Cargo capacity: 24,000 cubic feet
Main engine: MAK Diesel, 3,670 hp
Draft 14 feet
Surveyed by Det Norske Veritas

Island Mercy

Length: 173 feet
Breadth: 38 feet
Gross Tonnage: 998
Built: 1961 - Canada
Registered in Belize
Capacity: 60 berths

Cargo capacity: 12,680 cubic feet
Main engines. 2 Crossley diesel
(1,100 hp each)
Draft 12 feet, 6 inches
Surveyed by Lloyds

Pacific Ruby

Length: 140 feet
Breadth: 24 feet
Gross Tonnage: 488
Built: 1959 - Le Havre, France
Registered in Panama

Capacity: 35 berths
Main engines: 2 M60 diesel
electric drive (600 hp each)
Draft 11 feet

Chapter Seven

⟨ЖУЖ⟩

A Two-Edged Sword

⟨ЖУЖ⟩

Our deeds act upon us as much as we act upon them.
—George Eliot

VERONICA DIAZ and Naomi Benkert were glad the three days of dental screenings at the Princess Christian Maternity Hospital were over. The heat, the noise, and the smells, not to mention the life-affecting decisions that had to be made, all added to the physical and emotional strain of the work.

As Veronica filed away the last few records, a woman pushed through the dwindling crowd toward her. Standing squarely in front of Veronica, the woman silently unwrapped the bundle she was carrying to reveal a tiny, emaciated, three-year-old girl, whom she thrust into Veronica's arms. The woman looked belligerently into Veronica's eyes. "Pray for my daughter. She suffers too much," she demanded.

Veronica looked at the child in the woman's arms.

The little girl was weak, and her face and limbs were covered in huge scabs. Her half-opened eyes tried hard to focus. Veronica could see the girl teetering between life and death. She called Naomi over, and together they prayed for God's mercy and grace to come upon the small child.

As they were finishing their prayer, the mother interrupted them. "You must keep praying for my daughter. Her name is Tawah." She stared angrily at Veronica, who nodded and wrote Tawah's name in her prayer diary.

But the mother continued to be suspicious. "How will I know that you're not lying to me? How do I know you will really pray for her after I have gone? I need your address to keep checking up on you. You say you care, but do you really?"

The situation continued for several more minutes, with the mother being demanding and distrustful, while Veronica and Naomi tried to calm her fears.

Finally Tawah's mother made one last rude remark, bundled up her daughter, and left as quickly as she'd arrived.

That night, as Veronica went to pray, her heart was in turmoil. Two images vied for her attention. One image was of Tawah, who so desperately needed God's touch in her life. The other was of her pushy mother, who instead of asking for help, rudely demanded it.

Veronica struggled with her feelings toward the mother. The other people she had ministered to were so thankful and happy when they received help. But not Tawah's mother; she'd been rude and suspicious. With such an attitude, she hardly deserved any help. Yet her daughter's need was so obvious and so great.

Finally Veronica admitted her feelings to the Lord

and asked Him to help her deal with them. As she did so, the swirl of emotions she'd been feeling began to be replaced with feelings of compassion. She found that she was able to start to earnestly pray for the Lord to heal Tawah, and to minister to her mother, as well.

Veronica prayed that the Lord would remove the anger and bitterness from the mother's heart. The twin prayers remained on her lips throughout the next two months.

As the *Anastasis* medical crew prepared for their next screening at Princess Christian Maternity Hospital, Veronica was again assigned to the advance team.

Before the team even had a chance to set up their office, a woman propelled her way through the crowd toward them. She smiled broadly when she saw Veronica and waved a photograph at her. It was Tawah's mother.

"Soon after you prayed for my daughter, she got better. Now she is fine." With that she held the photo in front of Veronica's face. "Look. See. She is fine."

Veronica scanned the photograph for some point of familiarity, something that would bear a resemblance to the tiny, lifeless little person who had been thrust into her arms two months earlier. But there was none. The little girl in the photograph was standing and grinning from ear to ear. There were no scars, no marks, nothing to link her to the desperately ill child Veronica had seen.

And as Veronica looked up from the photograph of the new girl, she also saw a "new" mother. A week earlier the mother had received Christ into her life, and now she was filled with joy. Neither mother nor child were anything like the people she'd encountered two months earlier. Veronica's prayers had been answered—and then some!

Veronica had the joy of seeing her prayers answered, but she was only able to experience that joy because she passed the test. She had worked through her feelings toward Tawah's mother, which allowed her to pray earnestly for God's blessing on both mother and daughter.

At some time or another, each of us faces the same test Veronica faced. The circumstances may be different, but the test remains the same. The test occurs when we're confronted with a person in need and we have the resources to meet the need. Maybe the person needs friendship or compassion, perhaps material things or even physical healing. Whatever the need, we can meet it, and God asks us to do just that. But the person with the need is someone we're not sure is worthy of receiving our help. The attitude is demanding or belligerent, or we feel that the person is simply using us. Yet God asks us to meet the need. So the test becomes a struggle between our human emotions and obedience to what we know God has plainly told us to do.

Ananias was asked by the Lord to do something which brought him face to face with the same dilemma. Ananias was an early disciple who lived in the city of Damascus, and in a vision the Lord asked him to go to the house of Judas on Straight Street and pray for a man from Tarsus named Saul (Acts 9:11).

Of course, Ananias recognized this man as the dreaded persecutor of Christians, and immediately his human feelings came to the forefront. He made mention to the Lord of exactly who Saul was, hoping that the Lord may have overlooked the fact, and so cancel His directive. But the Lord simply restated His command for Ananias to go and pray for Saul. Now Ananias faced his test—obey God or give in to his feelings.

While Luke doesn't make reference to Ananias'

inner struggle, each of us can put ourselves in his place and sense what he would have felt. We can imagine how we would feel being asked to go and pray for the worst enemy of Christians at the time. Our very life could be in jeopardy as a result of following God's directive. After all, Saul had written authority from the Chief Priest to persecute and put to death Christians wherever he found them. And besides, it was doubtful if such a notorious person as Saul even deserved God's love and concern.

What would we have done?

What did Ananias do?

Ananias got up and went to find the house of Judas on Straight Street. There he found Saul—blind. As he prayed for Saul, scales fell from Saul's eyes and he was able to see again. After he had received his sight, he was baptized. The ministry of the apostle Paul had begun.

Ananias passed the test. And because he passed the test, he experienced the joy of being involved in the launching of the ministry of the Church's greatest apostle.

I'm sure God would have found someone else to pray for Saul if Ananias had chosen to disobey. But then Ananias would have missed out on the joyous blessing and the ensuing character growth that occurred as a result of his obedience.

I suppose that the next time the Lord asked Ananias to do something for Him, Ananias would have found the decision easier to make, because he already had this experience under his belt.

> Do not merely listen to the word, and so deceive yourselves. Do what it says. Anyone who listens to the word but does not do what it says is like a man who looks at his face in a

mirror and, after looking at himself, goes away and immediately forgets what he looks like. But the man who looks intently into the perfect law that gives freedom, and continues to do this, not forgetting what he has heard, but doing it—he will be blessed in what he does.

James 1:22-25

Hearing and doing. Not only do they bring us spiritual blessing, but they also build up our character so that we know beyond any doubt who it is we serve and why we serve Him. We become His instruments, and He shapes and molds us into what He wants us to be.

However, when we tell the Lord that we want to be an instrument in His hands, we had better be prepared for Him to guide us into places we might not choose to go, and to minister to people we might not choose to minister to. We better be able to lay aside our opinions in favor of God's injunctions, for when we give God permission to use us as His instrument, we also give Him permission to mold us and shape us into better, more useful instruments in His hands.

▸No Quick-Charge Holiness◂

At our Mercy Ships headquarters in Texas, one of the fun ways for the staff to get from building to building is by golf cart. On more than one occasion I have looked out to see would-be stock-car drivers blowing the cobwebs out of a golf cart as they race across the parking lot, or along the paths under the trees. The golf cart works fine all day, as long as we remember to plug it in at the end of the day so its batteries can recharge overnight.

How easy it would be if we could plug ourselves into an outlet as we slept at night and have our spiritual lives recharged with holiness! If only it were that easy!

Unfortunately it's not that easy. Holiness is active; it requires our cooperation to be shaped and molded by the various experiences of life. Holiness is not absorbed in the same way batteries absorb electricity. Instead, it is burned into our hearts and souls in the furnace of life.

> For he [God] will be like a refiner's fire or a launderer's soap. He will sit as a refiner and purifier of silver; he will purify the Levites and refine them like gold and silver. Then the Lord will have men who will bring offerings in righteousness.
>
> Malachi 3:2-3

Once we become Christians, God's primary interest focuses on developing our character and shaping us into His image. He becomes not only our Savior and Redeemer, but also our Refiner, shifting our heart away from those things that are not honoring or glorifying to Him. One of the fastest and most effective ways He does His refining work is to put us into situations where our flesh battles our spirit.

Of course, the prospect of such a struggle is not something most of us relish. But nonetheless, it is how God molds and shapes us into His image. So we should prepare ourselves for it.

The apostle Paul reminds us:

> But the fruit of the Spirit is love, joy, peace, patience, kindness, goodness, faithfulness, gentleness and self-control. Against such things there is no law. Those who belong to Christ Jesus have crucified the sinful nature with its passions and desires.
>
> Galatians 5:22-24

The person who exhibits the fruit of the Spirit is the person who has crucified, or dealt with, their sinful nature and all its passions and desires. They have laid aside their personal rights in order to embrace something far greater—the character of Christ flowing from them in the form of the fruits of the Spirit.

When we talk about the fruit of the Spirit, though, many of us think in passive terms. That is, we think that the more fruit we have, the more holy we will be.

Have you ever noticed what happens to juicy red apples if they're not picked? As they sit in the sun they start getting soft and mushy and begin rotting, until finally they fall to the ground and splatter. Apples were created to be eaten when they are fresh and ripe and crisp. When they are eaten like that, they nourish.

So it is with the fruit of the Spirit. The fruit of the Spirit is not something that should hang passively in our lives. Rather it is something that should be shared with others, nourishing them spiritually, physically, and emotionally.

James reminds us:

> What good is it, my brothers, if a man claims to have faith but has no deeds? Can such faith save him? Suppose a brother or sister is without clothes and daily food. If one of you says to him, "Go, I wish you well; keep warm and well fed," but does nothing about his physical needs, what good is it? In the same way, faith by itself, if it is not accompanied by action, is dead.
>
> James 2:14-17

Faith without action is dead. Thus, being a Christian demands some sort of demonstration of the fact on our part. We can't be closet Christians, because being a true Christian means that your faith will spill over into your actions. "For you died, and your life is now hidden with Christ in God," Paul tells us in Colossians 3:3. So our action flows out of Christ's character, not our own.

One life changed is that of Dr. Bob Dyer, one of the *Anastasis'* resident surgeons.

Dr. Dyer was a successful eye surgeon in San Diego, California, but his life came apart as his marriage ended and he lost his practice. He wound up working for the man who had bought his practice, and was thoroughly miserable.

One day he found a brochure on his desk describing Mercy Ships. He threw it away. A few weeks later, another brochure appeared; a hint, he suspected, from his daughter. He phoned for information and was invited to visit the *Anastasis* in Victoria, B.C., Canada.

After a tour of the ship and hearing of the plans for an eye surgery unit on board, Dr. Dyer agreed to draw up plans. Several months later, when the *Anastasis* was in California, Dr. Dyer found that the eye unit had been added—built to his specifications. But no eye doctor.

When he asked Dr. Christine Aroney-Sine, the M.D. aboard, who would run the clinic, she smiled.

"We don't have an eye surgeon yet. But we're going to Mexico in a few weeks. Would you like to come along?"

Dr. Dyer looked around the clinic—his clinic—and made a decision that changed his life.

In Mexico, Dr. Dyer performed eye surgery for poor people, people who could never afford his San Diego prices, people whose lives were forever changed by his skill. He had found a new purpose for his life.

After returning from Mexico, Dr. Dyer attended a Discipleship Training School. There he found a new depth of faith, and connected with God.

Returning to the *Anastasis* with only a few belongings— enough to fill his closet-sized cabin—Dr. Bob, as he is now known aboard ship, became an integral part of the crew.

According to Dr. Bob, the satisfaction of serving others is far greater than when he had a large practice with a large house and income. He recalls performing surgery on a little Senegalese boy who had been born blind due to cataracts.

During the post-operative exam the boy kept his head down and clung to his mother. He wouldn't look up. When Dr. Bob finally got a pair of glasses on the boy, he ducked his head again and then looked up in awe. He could see! "He did a double-take I will never forget. His face shone with all the wonder and awe of Christmas mornings, birthday parties, and Fourth of July fireworks rolled into one."

Today Dr. Bob enjoys working with short-term medical volunteers who take time off from their practices to join the ship in a port city.

"Everyone who goes into medicine has at least some desire to serve people. But when you start making money you lose some of those desires. When the volunteers see the impact they can make in someone's life in just an hour, it blows them away."

Many people who come on board—including Dr. Bob Dyer—say they've never been more fulfilled.

And what is the character of Christ that should flow from us? Jesus showed us what this character should be when He said:

> For I was hungry and you gave me something to eat, I was thirsty and you gave me something to drink, I was a stranger and you

invited me in, I needed clothes and you clothed
me, I was sick and you looked after me, I was in
prison and you came to visit me....I tell you the
truth, whatever you did for one of the least of
these brothers of mine, you did for me.

Matthew 25:35-40

Jesus covers here the gamut of suffering—the
thirsty, the hungry, the naked, the sick, the prisoner. In
reaching out to the sickest, the youngest, the most
hopeless of these people, He told the disciples that they
were in fact reaching out to Him. So ministering to the
poor, the suffering, and the needy is as close as we can
come to touching Christ here on earth. The closer we
get to such people, the more we show Him how much
we love Him and desire to be like Him.

The poor and the needy are like a mirror to our soul.
The way we respond to them is a measure of the depth
of our spiritual lives. Jesus spent much of His time on
earth ministering to such people. Do we? Or are we
inclined to think that holiness and spirituality are only
for display in church to other Christians?

I have wondered what Jesus meant when He told
the disciples that they would always have the poor with
them. When I hear the particular Scripture read aloud, it
is always done in a resigned, negative way. It is as though
whatever we do is not enough—it's only a drop in the
bucket, and the poor are always going to be around,
always needing help, always stretching our compassion
and willingness to give of ourselves.

But maybe Jesus didn't intend it to be a statement
of hopelessness. Perhaps He meant that the poor and
needy are always going to be around, because we need
them around to pry us free of our self-centeredness.
After all, when we reach out to the needy, we are reach-

ing out to the Lord. And whenever we touch Him, we are changed.

We will always have the poor with us; history attests to that fact. Yet God has specifically commanded us to minister to the poor and needy in His name. What are we to do? Should we obey the Lord? Should we follow the excuses we so quickly invent to allow us to remain focused on ourselves? Should we minister only to those we deem worthy of receiving our help? (Which is often very few, if any.) That is our test. What will we choose?

In facing this challenge, though, we must keep before us the fact that ministering to the poor and needy is a two-edged sword. Not only is the person in need helped, but in the process we are changed. Through our reaching out we are molded to be more like Jesus.

Down through history, the great leaders of the Church have been men and women whose characters have been shaped on the anvil of selfless giving of themselves to others.

For Veronica Diaz that anvil was Tawah's rude and abusive mother. Veronica could easily have returned to the M/V *Anastasis* and said to herself, "After the way that woman treated me, I'm not going to pray for her or her child. Who does she think she is to demand help in such a way? She's not worthy of the help she demands."

While Veronica may have had such feelings, that is not the course of action she followed. Instead, she gave her feelings to the Lord, and allowed Him to give her His compassion for Tawah and her mother. And for two months she gave herself to praying for them both. Her reward was not only the joy of seeing Tawah healed and her mother give her life to the Lord, it was also the spiritual growth that occurred in Veronica's life as a result.

Are we ready for the test? Are we ready to step out in obedience to God and start ministering to the poor and needy around us? Or are we content to listen to the fears and excuses of our heart and do nothing? The choice is ours, but we must choose carefully, because by making the wrong choice we are robbing ourselves of an opportunity to touch and minister to the Lord Jesus Himself. And touching the Lord Jesus always brings spiritual growth and holiness in our lives.

Chapter Eight

A Reward Awaits

HE WAS THE SON of a wealthy English-man, and was considered by many to be England's finest cricket player, having been the captain and best all-around player of the famed Cambridge University team. Yet wealth and athletic fame held little sway over him; his heart burned with a passion for the lost. And with that fire burning in his heart, C. T. Studd set out for China where for ten years he labored diligently, sharing the Gospel in the northern provinces until ill health forced him to return to England.

Even while recuperating, he traveled widely in the United States and Great Britain speaking and challenging Christians with the call to missions. Many thousands responded.

Despite his frequent poor health, Studd went on to serve as a missionary in India and Africa, and died in the Belgian Congo after a long and fruitful ministry.

Eric Liddell was also gifted with athletic prowess. He was one of the great athletes of the 1924 Olympics, where he won a gold medal in the 400-meter run. The story of his victory was told in the movie *Chariots of Fire*.

But like C. T. Studd, Liddell turned his back on fame and set his sights on serving God overseas. In 1925 he set out for China where he served as a missionary until 1945, when he died under house arrest by the occupying Japanese forces.

Jim Elliot was a man with a dream. His dream was to reach the Auca Indians, one of the most hostile tribes in all of South America, with the Gospel. With four others, he embarked upon Operation Auca, an ambitious plan to make contact with the Aucas and slowly introduce them to the Gospel.

For several months, the team dropped gifts to the Indians from their small Cessna airplane. The five finally landed in Auca territory on January 3, 1956. A small strip of sand alongside a river, which they had dubbed Palm Beach, served as their landing strip and base camp. But on the following Sunday, all five missionaries were attacked by the Aucas and killed.

A tragedy? Yes. But from that tragedy ultimately came victory. Jim Elliot's wife, Elizabeth, and Rachel Saint, sister of the group's pilot, Nate Saint, continued distributing gifts from the air to the Aucas. And finally, two years later, several Auca women emerged from the jungle and invited Rachel and Elizabeth to come and visit their village.

So began the evangelization of the Auca Indians.

Today, many of the Aucas are Christians. And they are Christians because of the sacrifice of Jim Elliot and his four co-workers.

C. T. Studd, Eric Liddell, Jim Elliot, and many

others like them in Church history were able to see beyond earthly values and embrace the eternal values of God's kingdom. They saw lost, hurting, dying people headed for a Christless eternity, and they determined in their hearts to do something about it.

They wanted to make their lives here on earth count for the kingdom of God. And the only way they knew how to do that was through obedience to the Lord's command to take the message of the Gospel to the ends of the earth and minister to people in Jesus' name. If that cost them fame and fortune—even their lives—they were prepared to make that sacrifice. Indeed, Jim Elliot's motto was: "He is no fool who gives what he cannot keep, to gain what he cannot lose."

Recently a sociologist interviewed a number of people who were 75 years of age or older. During the course of his interviews he asked these elderly people a simple question: "Looking back over your life, what would you have done differently?"

To the sociologist's surprise, two consistent responses to the question emerged. The first response was, "I would take more time to reflect." And the second, "I'd endeavor to do something of eternal value."

What interesting responses. People could have said, "I'd work harder to make more money, or better myself," or, "I'd organize my life differently so I had more leisure time." But no. These people would take more time to reflect and endeavor to do something of eternal value.

But perhaps their responses are not so surprising. All of us, when pressed, would probably give similar responses. Why? Because it is the way God has made us. He has created within us a religious dimension whose fulfillment is found in reflecting on life and its meaning.

Such reflection is intended to lead us ultimately to *the* Truth—God himself.

He has also placed within us a need for significance, a desire for what we do while on earth to add up to be more than the sum of its parts.

Solomon reminds us, "He [God] has also set eternity in the hearts of men" (Ecclesiastes 3:11).

As human beings we have been created with the notion of eternity firmly implanted within. And from that notion flows the need and desire to live for something that goes beyond our immediate, tangible needs.

That is what motivated C. T. Studd, Eric Liddell, and Jim Elliot. And it is why those elderly people questioned by the sociologist answered as they did. They realized that their departure into eternity was imminent, and they evaluated their lives in relation to it. They wondered if what they had done during their lifetime would last on past their death, or if they would soon be forgotten to become nameless faces in aging photographs in family albums.

All of us, young and old, can identify with their concern. We want our actions here on earth to survive our death and have some longer lasting significance to people.

However, the most startling thing about the responses of the people interviewed is the fact that they live in a world where frantic activity is the norm for most people. So the problem isn't that they're not doing anything, but that they're doing the wrong things. They are involved in things that don't have great significance and are not likely to account for much of eternal value. Perhaps that is why so many of them said they also wished they'd taken more time to reflect.

Taking the time to reflect is important for our

well-being as people. Reflecting gives us perspective. It allows us to disentangle our emotions and see things as they really are. Reflecting on the things we're doing with our lives is important, because it allows us to gauge the significance of the things we do in relation to eternity.

The story of Mary and Martha illustrates well how easily we can become entangled in busyness and miss those things which are important. Mary and Martha received Jesus into their home. But while Mary sat and listened to Jesus talk, Martha ran around trying to be the perfect hostess. When finally she complained to Jesus about Mary's lack of involvement in the preparations, He rebuked her. "Martha, Martha," the Lord answered, "you are worried and upset about many things, but only one thing is needed. Mary has chosen what is better, and it will not be taken away from her" (Luke 10:41-42).

What was better? Sitting at Jesus' feet and hearing what He had to say was better.

Martha's busyness may have produced results, perhaps a delicious spread of food on the table that Jesus could feast upon, but in the process she was missing doing the better, more important thing—sitting and listening to what Jesus had to say. The physical hunger of her guest may have been satisfied for a while as a result of her efforts, but her spiritual hunger would not have been. What she would receive from listening to Jesus would last long after He'd left her home.

So we must choose carefully the things that we do. It is easy to get sidetracked. I don't want to get to the end of my life and say, "I wish I'd spent more time reflecting on where my life was headed. I wish my life had had a more consistent game plan."

Jesus' life on earth offers us a clear example of how to apply our lives to works of eternal value. He constantly challenged the disciples to think beyond the mundane toward things that had eternal purpose and value. He challenged their motives for doing things, always prodding them to think about their priorities. It was probably an unnerving experience for the disciples, but Jesus didn't take things at surface value: He looked at the heart—from an eternal perspective.

Jesus' example is a reminder to us that we, too, should view our lives from an eternal perspective, and that all we do should be done with eternal values in mind. The greatest thing of eternal value we can do on earth is to be bearers of God's Good News to those who have not heard it.

❧We Seek a City❧

The writer to the Hebrews expressed the idea of searching after things of eternal value this way:

> For here we do not have an enduring city, but we are looking for the city that is to come. Through Jesus, therefore, let us continually offer to God a sacrifice of praise—the fruit of lips that confess his name. And do not forget to do good and to share with others, for with such sacrifices God is pleased.
>
> Hebrews 13:14-16

In 1983, while the *Anastasis* was ministering in the South Pacific island nation of Tonga, twenty-one-year-old Ofa Tanginoa came aboard as a student in our Discipleship Training School. Ofa had already completed two years of Bible college training, during which she had dedicated her life to reaching people in Africa with the Gospel.

After graduating from the Discipleship Training School she joined one of Mercy Ships' evangelism teams called South Sea Waves. This group of Pacific islanders employed their dynamic cultural dances to show the effects of the Gospel on their once-warring societies.

In 1987, South Sea Waves undertook a six-week ministry trip in Ghana and Kenya. For the first time, Ofa set foot on the continent she had dedicated her life to reaching with the Gospel. The trip was a tremendous success with many hundreds of Africans responding to the group's presentation and giving their lives to the Lord Jesus.

Several weeks into the trip, Ofa began to feel sick. What was first diagnosed as a viral infection turned out to be hepatitis and typhoid. At twenty-five years of age, on African soil, Ofa died.

Ofa Tanginoa had her eyes fixed firmly on the "city that is to come." Her one aim in life was to help as many others as possible, especially in Africa, to fix their eyes on that city as well.

Jesus said, "In my Father's house are many rooms; if it were not so, I would have told you. I am going there to prepare a place for you. And if I go and prepare a place for you, I will come back and take you to be with me that you also may be where I am" (John 14:2-3).

One of those rooms was for Ofa.

While family and co-workers still struggle with her loss, many hundreds of Africans have given their lives to the Lord as a result of hearing Ofa's story.

The things Ofa did during her life have had eternal value and significance long after her death. And that is what we are all striving for.

❧Lay Up Treasure❧

But store up for yourselves treasures in heaven, where moth and rust do not destroy, and where thieves do not break in and steal. For where your treasure is, there your heart will be also.

Matthew 6:20-21

Here Jesus touches on the other side of our desire to do things that are of lasting eternal value. In pursuing such things, we lay up for ourselves treasure in heaven.

Jesus added, "For the Son of Man is going to come in his Father's glory with his angels, and then he will reward each person according to what he has done" (Matthew 16:27).

And what are the deeds that are going to be rewarded?

In Luke's gospel Jesus gives us some insight.

But love your enemies, do good to them, and lend to them without expecting to get anything back. Then your reward will be great, and you will be sons of the Most High, because he is kind to the ungrateful and wicked. *Be merciful, just as your Father is merciful.* [Italics mine.]

Luke 6:35-36

God's promised rewards, both now and in eternity, are for those who live a life of mercy and compassion.

The writer of Proverbs 21:13 tells us: "If a man shuts his ears to the cry of the poor, he too will cry out and not be answered."

Being kind and merciful to those who are in need is not an optional extra that we Christians can choose to do if we so please. Rather, it is to be at the center of our actions. No matter where we are, we are to think first of those who are in need, those who cry out to us.

Sometimes I don't think we fully comprehend how much the poor and needy of this world are on God's heart. But I trust that as you read this book you'll begin to see the special place they hold in His heart. As His sons and daughters, we must realize that our response to the poor and needy is very important.

How seriously do we take our responsibility to be merciful? It was, after all, Jesus who said, "Blessed are the merciful, for they will be shown mercy" (Matthew 5:7).

We must *give* mercy in order to receive it. It's that simple.

We can embark on a short-term mission trip to teach hygiene to a primitive people, become involved in a feeding program for the homeless, give money to restore the eyesight of a blind child, or bring a needy family into our home while they get on their feet again. All these are ways in which we can accomplish the Lord's admonition to be merciful.

Jesus promised to reward each act of mercy. "And if anyone gives a cup of cold water to one of these little ones because he is my disciple, I tell you the truth, he will certainly not lose his reward" (Matthew 10:42).

On the last day, I do not want to be looking back at things I could have done for others, but left undone through selfishness or thoughtlessness. I want to have laid up for myself treasure in heaven through my actions while here in this world. This life gives us one opportunity to set the stage for eternity, and we need to be very careful about how we use that opportunity.

Keith Green recounts an interesting story in *A Cry in the Wilderness*. The story concerns a beggar in India who had been out begging all day for food and money. By day's end all he had to show for his efforts was half a cup of rice. Just as he was about to go and find somewhere to sleep for the night, he noticed a crowd beginning to form.

The prince was coming!

So the beggar spread out his mat again and sat down to await the spectacle. Several minutes went by, then the prince came into view riding on an elephant. When the prince saw the beggar, he ordered the elephant to stop. He climbed down and walked over to the poor man. A crowd gathered around them as the prince asked the beggar for some of his rice.

The beggar didn't know what to do. On the one hand he was angry that a prince—a man who had so much—would demand his tiny dinner. But if he gave the prince nothing, he could well find himself in the royal jail. So begrudgingly the beggar counted out three grains of rice and gave them to the prince.

The prince thanked the beggar, climbed back onto his elephant, and went on his way. As the prince left, his head servant walked over to the beggar and counted out three gold coins—one for each grain of rice—and tossed them into the beggar's lap.

Of course, the beggar was mortified. If only he had given the prince all of his rice—how rich he would have been! He wanted to run after the prince and give him every grain of rice he had. But it was too late; the prince's caravan had moved on.

> He who is kind to the poor lends to the Lord, and he will reward him for what he has done.
>
> Proverbs 19:17

When we lend something to someone there is an expectation that we will be repaid. And according to the writer of the Proverbs, when we are kind to the poor we lend to the Lord. God Himself stands behind the promise of repaying us for whatever we give, be it our time, talent, or money.

Every single thing we give in Jesus' name will be repaid to us, perhaps not in this life, but most certainly in the life to come. If God says He will repay us, then He will.

The God who owns the cattle on a thousand hills asks us to give the little we have to those who are the most needy among us. But so often we want to hold back. We rationalize and tell ourselves that what we have to offer is too small an offering and will not really help, or we worry that if we give of our time, talent, or money it may go unnoticed and unrewarded. How wrong we are.

Everything that we do, every sacrificial act, every kind deed, every comforting word, is recorded in heaven. It is laid up for us as treasure, to be given to us on that wondrous day when we enter the gates of heaven into the presence of the living God.

Some people give much but get back even more. Others don't give what they should and end up poor. Whoever gives to others will get richer; those who help others will themselves be helped.

Proverbs 11:24-25, New Century Version

Each of us can give that which we cannot keep to gain that which we cannot lose. Along the way we not only lay up for ourselves treasure in heaven and participate in something of eternal value, but we also have the privilege of participating with God in ministering to the lives of needy and hurting people. And above that, there is no greater joy.

Chapter Nine

How Shall We Then Live?

Always preach the Gospel; use words when necessary.
—Saint Francis of Assisi

THE TITLE OF Francis Schaeffer's film series, *How Shall We Then Live?*, asks the ultimate question. Given all that we know, all that we believe, all that we are striving to be, how shall we then live?

In the strictest sense, no one can tell us exactly how we should live, since God has a unique path for each of us to follow. But beyond the unique path that God has for each of us, there are certain requirements the Word of God addresses which should mark the way people are to live their lives as Christians.

Some of those requirements have to do with mercy and compassion. If we are born again into God's family, He asks each of us to be conduits through which His love can flow to the hurting and downtrodden of this world.

Again, we come back to the question: How shall we live in order to accomplish this?

I trust that through this book you've begun to see some of the things you can do in your life that will help you become more practically concerned about and involved with the plight of the poor and needy in our world. The following are some practical ways in which we can be faithful to the Lord in dispensing His love and compassion to others.

Be Present

With it he touched my mouth and said, "See, this has touched your lips; your guilt is taken away and your sin atoned for." Then I heard the voice of the Lord saying, "Whom shall I send? And who will go for us?" And I said, "Here am I. Send me!"

Isaiah 6:7-8

As Christians, we have the words of hope which so many people in our world desperately need to hear. If we do nothing else, we can simply be physically present among those who need to see and to hear the life-changing message of the Gospel.

I'm sure all of us, at some time or another, have felt totally inadequate when a friend or relative faced grief or tragedy. We felt uncomfortable not knowing what to do or say. But to our amazement, after the crisis had passed, the person has come and said to us, "Thank you for just being there."

As human beings, we have been designed to derive comfort from merely knowing that another person is with us in spirit, and that they understand or are trying to understand what we're going through.

We can do the same for spiritually hurting and

grieving people, too. Our physical presence, whether helping to referee a basketball game for at-risk inner city youth, or feeding the starving in Africa, is invaluable. People begin to understand that we really care about them when they see us willingly give up our rights to comfort and recreation in order to be with them and help them in their need.

Jesus did not save us so we could cut ourselves off from the world. He saved us to be His representatives in it. We are to be His salt and light.

> The one who sowed the good seed is the Son of Man. The field is the world, and the good seed stands for the sons of the kingdom....The harvest is the end of the age, and the harvesters are angels.
>
> Matthew 13:37-39

We are the seeds that Jesus has sown in the world. It is our job to grow and bring forth good fruit for the harvest.

Christianity isn't about adhering to rules; it's about an exchanged life, a life that is compelled by God's love, not self-interest. The greatest witness to the world of God's existence and His love for all people is the practically expressed love Christians have for other people.

Christianity is not about elaborate rituals and expensive buildings; it's about going among the people and demonstrating God's practical love. "Dear children, let us not love with words or tongue but with actions and in truth" (I John 3:18).

A good first action is simply being there for people.

❧Be Faithful❧

I heard the story of an elderly woman who attended a Christian teaching series on discovering your spiritual giftings. Instead of shedding light on the subject, the woman found it all very confusing.

Eventually she went to her pastor to find out exactly what her spiritual gift might be. The wise pastor posed a simple question: "What do you like to do?"

The woman thought for a few moments. What did she like to do? She tried to think of something very spiritual, but she couldn't. So she blurted out the only thing she could think of, "I make pretty good soup."

The pastor smiled at her and said, "Well, then, make soup." It seemed strange advice for a spiritual man to give her, but she respected the pastor and did what he had told her.

The first thing she did upon arriving home was make a list of people she knew who were either sick or in need of encouragement. Then she made soup: chicken soup, vegetable soup, bean soup—every kind of soup you could imagine. Her mission was to deliver soup to everyone on her list at least once a week.

Over the next several months, the woman noticed an interesting change. As she brought them soup, people began to chat with her about their concerns. Some stopped her for wise counsel. Others needed her encouragement, or simply asked her to pray for them. Through her homespun hospitality, many of her neighbors began to open up their lives to her and to the Gospel.

Excited by what she saw happening in the lives of the people she took her soup to, the woman went back to visit her pastor. "You were right," she told him, "Making soup is a spiritual gift! I've got a new motto: Love them till they ask you why!"

There is a valuable lesson for us all in this woman's story. Mercy can be many things. It can be pulling a boat person from shark-infested waters, or it can be a skilled physician operating on the tumorous growth of a child in Africa. More often, though, it is something considerably less spectacular, like making soup!

It's unimportant whether or not an act of mercy appears spectacular or not. What is important is that true mercy is offered in the name of the Lord.

And when such mercy is offered without strings attached, it inevitably leads people to ask the obvious question: "Why are you doing this for me?"

Experience teaches us that most often it is not the big things we do that make a lasting impression on people, but the small things.

If we are faithful to use the gifts God has given us for the good of others, our actions will have a lasting impact upon the lives of others.

✍ Be Equipped ✍

May the God of peace...equip you with everything good for doing his will, and may he work in us what is pleasing to him, through Jesus Christ, to whom be glory for ever and ever. Amen.

Hebrews 13:20-21

We live in a very troubled world, and God wants to reach out to that world through each of us. In order to do so, He wants to equip us with everything we will need. The question is: Are we willing to have God reshape our lives, our goals, and our priorities in order to be equipped to accomplish all He has for us to do?

After reading this book, I challenge each person to set aside a day for prayer and fasting. During this time ask the Lord, "What is it You would have me do to bring hope and healing to this suffering world? And what are the steps I need to take to equip myself for that task?"

An obvious step we can all take to equip ourselves is to develop a solid knowledge of God's Word. "All scripture is God-breathed and is useful for teaching, rebuking, correcting and training in righteousness, so that the man of God may be thoroughly equipped for every good work" (II Timothy 3:16-17).

We shouldn't usually wait until we see a need to figure out how we can equip ourselves to meet that need. Equipping should take place before we go out to minister to the poor and needy.

Imagine if you were to have a heart attack. Who would we want beside us? Would we want someone already skilled in CPR, or someone who intends to study it as soon as the need arises? There is no doubt who we would want—the skilled person.

Over the years I have spoken to many people who have told me, "I felt God wanted me to study to be a doctor [or nurse or medical technician], but I got sidetracked. I wish I'd made the sacrifices at the time, because now I see such need."

Well, the good news is that God is a God of redemption. He always has something good in store for us, no matter how many detours we may make. The important thing is not to look back at missed opportunities, but to look forward to all that God has for us and all that He can do through us. With that vision squarely in sight, we can plan accordingly and fully equip ourselves for future ministry to the poor and needy.

❧Be Prayerful☙

> The prayer of a righteous man is powerful and effective. James 5:16

Too often today we underestimate the power of our prayers. We think that praying is a kind of second-rate

Christian service. In reality, prayer is a vital link between God and man.

Prayer knows no physical boundaries. God is just as able to intervene in a person's life whether he's half-way around the world or lives in our neighborhood. When Christians mobilize and focus their prayers on areas of great need, things do happen!

Consider the former Soviet Union. A few short years ago, who would have thought that Christian ministries would have free access into a country that was once a dictatorial Communist/Atheist state? And who would have thought that freedom of religion would be part of the constitution of a new Russia?

But people prayed for those things to happen, and at the appointed time, they occurred. God opened the doors of closed countries so His light could shine in.

As Christians we need to form the habit of responding to the needs of our world with immediate prayer. Imagine the tremendous impact if instead of rushing to the television, Christian families opened the newspaper and spent fifteen minutes praying together for one or several of the needy situations presented in it.

When anyone shares a prayer concern with one active intercessor I know, she says, "Okay, let's pray about it right now." This comes as quite a shock to some Christians who expect her to go and pray about their need in the quiet of her home.

"You mean pray right now? Here?" I've heard them sputter. But why not? The prayer of a righteous person is powerful, and the needs of our world require powerful responses.

✐Be Generous but Wise✐

One of the marks of a mature believer is putting

love into action through financial giving. Indeed, the ministry I lead, Mercy Ships, is sustained by the generous contributions of God's committed people. They have caught the vision of extending His mercy by using ships adapted and equipped with the necessary resources to respond to a wide range of needs. And because these people have caught the vision, they have become partners, contributing regularly to see that the mission of Mercy Ships moves forward.

I also know that many of those who financially support Mercy Ships do so sacrificially. They do not give out of their excess. Instead, they forego things and make sacrifices in order to be able to give. They are our partners, each one investing a part of himself into our ministry.

However, while as Christians we're to be known as giving people, the Lord Jesus also reminds us that we are to be as wise as serpents but as innocent as doves. This means that while we are to give, we also need to be wise about what it is we give to. In the wake of the numerous scandals that have rocked the Body of Christ in recent years, we need to be sure that what we are giving is being used wisely in the furthering of God's kingdom.

Recently I was invited to a conference in Costa Rica, along with the heads of every major Christian relief and development organization in the world. The underlying theme of the conference was, "What's Christian about Christian relief and development?" And it is a very good question for every Christian and every ministry to ask themselves from time to time.

The Christian businessman who funded and organized the conference did so as a result of observing many relief projects around the world which he had personally funded. He told us how, through the auspices of a

Christian relief organization, he had invested one million dollars into a project to bring fresh drinking water to the Waloff people of Senegal.

But at a ceremony held to thank the organization for drilling the many water wells, he was shocked. Jesus wasn't mentioned once at the event. The children sang songs to Muhammed and extolled the virtues of Islam. The man's money had been given in the name of the Lord Jesus to bring relief to these people, and they had not even been made aware of why it was they were receiving fresh water. He told us how grieved he was about the incident. Over a million dollars had been spent, and not one single person had heard the name of Jesus or had their world view challenged!

Now there is nothing wrong with humanitarian efforts to help people. But it is disappointing to see Christian organizations raising large sums of money within the Body of Christ and then dispersing it without even making it known that it was being given in the name of Jesus.

So while we should be generous givers to the ongoing work of the Lord, including mercy and relief work, we should know exactly who and what we are giving to, and be satisfied that the money will be used in such a way so as to lift up the name of the Lord among those who receive the benefit from it.

We should also look to long-term, ongoing ministry. Most of us want the money we give to Christian relief organizations not only to bring relief to the immediate needs, but also to be a catalyst to see people won to the Lord and to see churches planted among them.

As the leader of a Christian relief ministry, I know how easy it is to get overwhelmed and sidetracked by the obvious and immediate needs of people. But the most obvious need is not usually the person's deepest need—the deepest need is most often spiritual.

We are called to deliver the "two-handed" Gospel my mother told me about: a hand of practical concern and help, and a hand of spiritual care and guidance. It is all too easy to overlook this second hand and not properly address the spiritual needs of people. But the spiritual need is most important. We should be guiding them into the hope that is found only in Jesus Christ.

As mature sons and daughters of the living God, we must seek out and support those ministries and organizations within the Body of Christ who dispense the full two-handed Gospel.

It should also be noted that generous giving starts as an act of the heart before it becomes an amount. God isn't as interested in the amount we give as He is in the spirit in which we give it. And when we give with a pure heart, He is able to take what we give and multiply it.

That is the message from the miracle of the feeding of the five thousand. One small boy generously gave his meager lunch of loaves and fishes to Jesus, and Jesus multiplied it to feed the gathered crowd. That is how God does things. He causes exponential growth. In our commitment to the ongoing work of mercy and relief, God will take what we give and multiply it for His glory.

❧Be a Doer of Good Works❧

Let your light shine before men, that they may see your good deeds and praise your Father in heaven.

Matthew 5:16

Good works. Something in us almost wants to push these two words away, as though they're dangerous. In the wake of the Reformation, the Church has often gone to great lengths to avoid anything that might look as though we're trying to earn our salvation. In so doing we have down-played the responsibility and privilege that is ours to practically show God's love to the world.

As a result, we tend to expect the government to feed the hungry, house the homeless, and provide health care for the sick. Sure, a government has certain responsibilities to take care of its citizens. But when Christians abdicate their responsibility to do good works, people are robbed of the opportunity to hear about God and to glorify Him. Without compassionate actions to back up our words, the Gospel has little opportunity to touch the hearts of unbelieving and hurting people. As James reminds us, faith without works is dead.

But there is hope. Good works are slowly beginning to take hold in the evangelical Church. Some churches are establishing homes for unwed mothers, feeding programs for street people, or shelters for the homeless. In the Body of Christ, love and compassion are beginning to become more than words—they are becoming a lifestyle that flows from a living and dynamic faith.

Ed is a great example of this new lifestyle. Ed is a husband, father, and president of the Board of Elders in his local church. He is also a full-time social worker by day. Through his local church, Ed has initiated a program to feed homeless people in the community. For more than two years, he has given three or four nights a week to make sure hungry people are fed a hot meal and told about God's love. Ed has also helped another man open a discipleship home for street people who have committed their lives to Christ.

Is Ed going to be saved because of all the good works he is doing? No. But other people are being saved as a result of his good deeds.

Jesus told His disciples that when they fed, clothed, or visited someone in need, they were doing those things to Him. That is our catalyst for action. That is what should guide us forward in ministering to the needs of people. When we touch people and meet their needs, we are touching and ministering to the Lord Jesus Himself.

ᴖ How Shall We Then Live? ᴕ

For me, there is no question. The issue was settled as I grew up in western Colorado. From earliest memory, my parents showed me what it meant to be a Christian and to be concerned for the poor and needy.

On Saturday evenings my mother would prepare "care packages" full of family necessities such as vegetables, baby clothes, soap, and canned goods. On Sunday mornings my dad would load the packages into the trunk of the car and off we'd head for church—but not by the fastest route.

Mom would direct Dad to a variety of homes where she knew there were needs. At each house she would get a box from the trunk and take it in. As she handed over the care package she would invite the children to Sunday School.

More often than not, they would accept her offer, and my brother and I rolled our eyes and groaned as we squeezed closer to make room for the extra kids in the back seat. If we ever complained to my mother about the inconvenience or the overcrowding, she would always say the same thing, "The Lord gave us two hands—one to reach down and help our neighbor and the other to give him the Gospel."

It may seem simplistic, but it is the principle upon which I have based my Christian life and ministry. It is a principle that works. In western Colorado today, there are people who are Christians because of the efforts of my mom and dad. Each one of those people is a testimony to the effectiveness of the two-handed Gospel.

But more than that, the two-handed Gospel is the pattern of life which the Lord Jesus modeled for us to follow. He was always greatly concerned about the spiritual needs of the people He came in contact with. At the same time, He was also deeply concerned about their physical needs. And He never addressed the one need without also addressing the other.

That is how we should live!

My prayer is that after reading this book, you too will be challenged to follow the example of the Lord Jesus and begin to dispense the Gospel with both hands. More than at any time in our history, we are overwhelmed by human suffering and tragedy. The world is desperate for the tender, gentle, merciful touch of the Lord Jesus Christ, administered through the hearts and hands of His faithful followers—you and me.

Endnotes

1—Ruth Tucker, *From Jerusalem to Irian Jaya* (Grand Rapids, Michigan: Academie Books, 1983), 26.

2—Tucker, 27.

3—F. F. Bruce, *The Spreading Flame* (Grand Rapids, Michigan: Wm. B. Eerdmans Publishing Company, 1958), 191.

4—Kenneth Scott Latourette, *A Christian History, Volume 1: Beginnings to 1500* (New York: Harper and Row, 1953), 558.

5—Bruce, 191.

6—Philip Yancey, *I Was Just Wondering* (Grand Rapids, Michigan: Wm. B. Eerdmans Publishing Company, 1989), 102.

7—Tucker, 241.

8—Keith Green, *A Cry in the Wilderness* (Nashville, Tennessee: Sparrow Press, 1993), 110.

9—Green, 109.

10—Gray Temple, Jr., *52 Ways to Help Homeless People* (Nashville, Tennessee: Oliver Nelson, 1991), 21.

Appendix

Caring for the Poor and Needy

1. God's View of the Poor and Needy

Key Verses	Main Focus
Psalm 102:17—"He will respond to the prayer of the destitute; he will not despise their plea."	God hears and responds
Proverbs 22:22-23—"Do not exploit the poor because they are poor and do not crush the needy in court, for the Lord will take up their case and will plunder those who plunder them."	God defends
Jeremiah 20:13—"Sing to the Lord! Give praise to the Lord! He rescues the life of the needy from the hands of the wicked."	God rescues
Isaiah 25:4—"You have been a refuge for the poor, a refuge for the needy in his distress, a shelter from the storm and a shade from the heat."	God is their refuge

God gives them
great faith

James 2:2-9—"Suppose a man comes into your meeting wearing a gold ring and fine clothes, and a poor man in shabby clothes also comes in. If you show special attention to the man wearing fine clothes and say, 'Here's a good seat for you,' but say to the poor man, 'You stand there' or 'Sit on the floor by my feet,' have you not discriminated among yourselves and become judges with evil thoughts?

"Listen, my dear brothers: Has not God chosen those who are poor in the eyes of the world to be rich in faith and to inherit the kingdom he promised those who love him? But you have insulted the poor. Is it not the rich who are exploiting you? Are they not the ones who are dragging you into court? Are they not the ones who are slandering the noble name of him to whom you belong?

"If you really keep the royal law found in Scripture, 'Love your neighbor as yourself,' you are doing right. But if you show favoritism, you sin and are convicted by the law as lawbreakers."

2. Our Responsibility to Them

Main Focus

Lend freely

Key Verses

Matthew 5:42—"Give to the one who asks you, and do not turn away from the one who wants to borrow from you."

Leviticus 25:35-37—"If one of your countrymen becomes poor and is unable to support himself among you, help him as you would an alien or a temporary resident, so he can continue to live among you.

"Do not take interest of any kind from him, but fear your God, so that your countryman may continue to live among you. You must not lend him money at interest or sell him food at a profit."

Make no profit off them

Jeremiah 22:11-17—"For this is what the Lord says about Shallum son of Josiah, who succeeded his father as king of Judah but has gone from this place: 'He will never return. He will die in the place where they have led him captive; he will not see this land again.

Defend them

"'Woe to him who builds his palace by unrighteousness, his upper rooms by injustice, making his countrymen work for nothing, not paying them for their labor. He says, "I will build myself a great palace with spacious upper rooms." So he makes large windows in it, panels it with cedar and decorates it in red.

"'Does it make you a king to have more and more cedar? Did not your father have food and drink? He did what was right and just, so all went well with him. He defended the cause of the poor and needy, and so all went well. Is that not what it means to know me?' declares the Lord. 'But your eyes and your heart are set only on dishonest gain, on shedding innocent blood and on oppression and extortion.'"

Give generously

Psalm 37:25-26—"I was young and now I am old, yet I have never seen the righteous forsaken or their children begging bread. They are always generous and lend freely; their children will be blessed."

Notice their plight and take action

I John 3:16-18—"This is how we know what love is: Jesus Christ laid down his life for us. And we ought to lay down our lives for our brothers. If anyone has material possessions and sees his brother in need but has no pity on him, how can the love of God be in him? Dear children, let us not love with words or tongue, but with actions and in truth."

Proverbs 21:13—"If a man shuts his ears to the cry of the poor, he too will cry out and not be answered."

Ezekiel 16:49—"Now this was the sin of your sister Sodom: She and her daughters were arrogant, overfed and unconcerned; they did not help the poor and needy."

Show kindness

Proverbs 14:21,31—"He who despises his neighbor sins, but blessed is he who is kind to the needy. He who oppresses the poor shows contempt for their Maker, but whoever is kind to the needy honors God."

Matthew 25:35-45—"'For I was hungry and you gave me something to eat, I was thirsty and you gave me something to drink, I was a stranger and you invited me in, I needed clothes and you clothed me, I was sick and you looked after me, I was in prison and you came to visit me.'

"Then the righteous will answer him, 'Lord, when did we see you hungry and feed you, or thirsty and give you something to drink? When did we see you a stranger and invite you in, or needing clothes and clothe you? When did we see you sick or in prison and go to visit you?'

"The King will reply, 'I tell you the truth, whatever you did for one of the least of these brothers of mine, you did for me.'

"Then he will say to those on his left, 'Depart from me, you who are cursed, into the eternal fire prepared for the devil and his angels. For I was hungry and you gave me nothing to eat, I was thirsty and you gave me nothing to drink, I was a stranger and you did not invite me in, I needed clothes and you did not clothe me, I was sick and in prison and you did not look after me.'

"They also will answer, 'Lord, when did we see you hungry or thirsty or a stranger or needing clothes or sick or in prison, and did not help you?'

Share and provide for

"He will reply, 'I tell you the truth, whatever you did not do for one of the least of these, you did not do for me.'

"Then they will go away to eternal punishment, but the righteous to eternal life."

3. God's Response

Main Focus   *Key Verses*

A. To those who oppress:

God judges

Amos 8:4-12—"Hear this, you who trample the needy and do away with the poor of the land, saying, 'When will the New Moon be over that we may sell grain, and the Sabbath be ended that we may market wheat?'— skimping the measure, boosting the price and cheating with dishonest scales, buying the poor with silver and the needy for a pair of sandals, selling even the sweepings with the wheat.

"The Lord has sworn by the Pride of Jacob: 'I will never forget anything they have done. Will not the land tremble for this, and all who live in it mourn? The whole land will rise like the Nile; it will be stirred up and then sink like the river of Egypt.

"'In that day,' declares the Sovereign Lord, 'I will make the sun go down at noon and darken the earth in broad daylight. I will turn your religious feasts into mourning and all your singing into weeping. I will make all of you wear sackcloth and shave your heads. I will make that time like mourning for an only son and the end of it like a bitter day.

"'The days are coming,' declares the Lord, 'when I will send a famine throughout the land—not a famine of food or a thirst for water, but a famine of hearing the words of the Lord. Men will stagger from sea to sea and wander from north to east, searching for the word of the Lord, but they will not find it.'"

Proverbs 17:5—"He who mocks the poor shows contempt for their Maker; whoever gloats over disaster will not go unpunished."

God punishes

Proverbs 21:13—"If a man shuts his ears to the cry of the poor, he too will cry out and not be answered."

God ignores their cries

Psalm 72:4—"He will defend the afflicted among the people and save the children of the needy; he will crush the oppressor."

God crushes

B. To those who bless:

Key Verses

Main Focus

Psalm 112:5—"Good will come to him who is generous and lends freely, who conducts his affairs with justice."

God will come to them

Proverbs 19:17—"He who is kind to the poor lends to the Lord, and he will reward him for what he has done."

God will reward them

God will provide for them

Proverbs 28:27—"He who gives to the poor will lack nothing, but he who closes his eyes to them receives many curses."

God will bless, deliver, protect, preserve, sustain, and restore health

Psalm 41:1-3—"Blessed is he who has regard for the weak; the Lord delivers him in times of trouble. The Lord will protect him and preserve his life; he will bless him in the land and not surrender him to the desire of his foes. The Lord will sustain him on his sickbed and restore him from his bed of illness."

Questions for Further Study

Chapter One:
Seeing the World through Different Eyes

1. Think of a recent major disaster.
   a. What were some of your initial reactions to it?
   b. Can you see those reactions reflected in the four world views outlined by the author?
2. Why do you think the parable of the Good Samaritan has become the most well-known parable of all time?
3. Give some examples of Christians that you know personally, or by reputation, who are examples of compassion and mercy to this generation.
4. List what you would consider to be the major hindrances to you in exhibiting a greater degree of mercy and compassion to others.
5. When we explain our Christian journey, we often speak in terms of our past, present, and future hope. Very briefly, give your testimony in those terms.
6. Explain several differences that would exist in your life if your language and cultural background had no concept or word for "future." What are some limitations this would place upon you?

Chapter Two: *Echoes of Mercy*

1. In the example of Iris and baby Wanda, what positive effects did the offering of mercy have, even though Wanda died?

2. How often do you allow the probable outcome of your merciful actions to dictate whether or not you proceed with those acts?

3. Describe a time when someone reached out to you in mercy and it had a lasting effect on your life. What was it about the incident that touched you most?

4. Jesus told the disciples, "Freely you have received, freely give." Make a list of the things that you have received from God in your life.

5. Alongside your list, check the things that you freely offer to others.

6. During the outbreak of plague in ancient Alexandria, Christians are documented as having risked their own lives to tend to dying heathens. What do you think motivated them? What impact might this have had on those they reached out to?

7. In the author's illustration about the three blind men and the elephant, several means of spreading the Gospel are mentioned. Which one do you feel you engage in most regularly? Why?

Chapter Three: *Hindrances to Mercy*

1. Why do we find it so much easier to judge others than to judge ourselves?

2. In a Christian context, are some people more or less deserving of mercy than others? Explain your answer, giving examples from the life of Jesus.

3. What type of people do you write off as being undeserving of your mercy?

4. When it comes to extending mercy to others, why is the concept of "a future hope" important?

5. How is feeling sorry for someone often confused with mercy? Why do you think this happens?

6. The author states, "Mercy is like a lens that focuses the light of eternity on a person's need." What do you think is meant by that statement? Have you or someone you know experienced this?

7. In your own experience have you found a personal balance between meeting local and global needs? Share how you found that balance, or how you think you could find it in the future.

Chapter Four: *One to One*

1. List the ways in which this generation is more informed about tragic personal situations or large-scale disasters than previous generations have been.

2. Are there times when you feel overwhelmed by the media coverage of disastrous events? How does this affect the way you react to them?

3. What would you like to do to alleviate some area of suffering in the world today?

4. In practical terms, what steps could you take toward achieving that goal?

5. Have you ever been in a situation where you felt you were judged in some stereotypical way, and not on who you really were? Discuss the situation and how it made you feel. How do you think your attitudes would change if you were consistently made to feel unimportant because of circumstances beyond your control?

6. When you see a large group of people suffering, such as in a war or famine, what can you do to remind yourself that this group is made up of many individual people with their own needs and concerns?

Chapter Five: *Partnership with God*

1. Can you think of a time when you did something which seemed small or insignificant, but which God imbued with more significance?

2. Why is it so important to follow the Holy Spirit's leading rather than our own logic when it comes to showing mercy and compassion?

3. Jesus said of the man born blind, "...but this has happened so that the work of God can be displayed in his life." How can we be a part of showing the work of God in other people's lives?

4. "Between the great things we cannot do and the little things we will not do, the danger is that we will do nothing."

   a. What are the great things which we cannot do at the moment?

   b. What are some of the little things that we are able to do but don't?

   c. Why don't we do those things?

   d. What are some acts of mercy or compassion that are within our reach?

   e. When and how can we begin to carry them out?

Chapter Six: *Valuing Value*

1. Name some groups of people who are generally valued less by society. What situations or events are most likely to make one person seem of less value than another?

2. Name a situation or event that could happen to you in the next twenty-four hours that would have the potential to decrease your value in the eyes of others. How would you react to this change in status?

3. Give three examples of ways in which Jesus deliberately reached out to reinforce the value of a person when the society in which they lived did not value them.

4. Name some of the reactions people might have toward us if we reached out across the invisible boundaries to treat the needy with respect.

5. Gray Temple, Jr., suggests that one of the best ways to validate people is to enjoy their company. Why would this be true, and how does it change the person?

6. Can you think of a time when you reassessed the value you placed on a person once you saw how others valued them?

7. How can the way we treat a person lead others to reassess the way they treat them?

Chapter Seven: A Two-Edged Sword

1. What might prevent a person in need from having a good attitude toward those who might be able to meet that need?

2. Do you always find it easy to receive from others and to express gratefulness to them? If not, why not?

3. Think of a time recently when you struggled with the attitude of someone you felt God wanted you to help. Did you end up helping them? Why or why not?

4. Jesus said that when we reach out to the neediest and the poorest among us, we are really reaching out to Him. What do you think He meant by that? What are the practical implications for our lives today?

5. In thinking about Mother Teresa, we are familiar with the impact she has had on the poor in India. But what effect do you think the poor might have had on her over the course of her lifetime?

6. If a Christian is not receiving spiritual sustenance and trying to live by the principles of mercy and compassion, what is likely to happen to them? Have you ever been in that situation?

Chapter Eight: A Reward Awaits

1. The author refers to a group of elderly people who had two regrets: (1) They would like to have taken more time to reflect, and (2) they would have liked to have done something of eternal value. At your stage of life, how do you relate to those statements?

2. List the goals that you have set for your life. What categories do they fall into? (e.g., career, relationships, etc.).

3. Do you feel you have a good balance of spiritual goals?

4. Ecclesiastes 3:11 states, "He has also set eternity in the hearts of men," and the author states, "As human beings we have been created with the notion of eternity firmly implanted within. And from that notion flows the need and desire to live for something that goes beyond our immediate, tangible needs." Do you agree with those statements? If so, in what ways do you see them through your own experience?

5. Why do you think there is such a struggle between the desire to do something of eternal value and the desire for comfort and security?

6. Suggest several things we could do to help us overcome that struggle within us.

Chapter Nine: How Shall We Then Live?

1. What impact can you have by merely being present with the poor and needy?

2. The author states, "Christianity isn't about adhering to rules, it's about an exchanged life." What do you think he means by that?

3. In an illustration in this chapter, the pastor tells the elderly woman that in order to practice her spiritual gift she should go and make soup. What is it that you could do? Where could you practice that gift?

4. The author contends that often the small things people do for us make the most impression. Can you think of a time when this was true in your own experience?

5. In which direction do you think God might be leading you? What are you doing now to prepare for that? What else could you be doing?

6. What criteria would you use to evaluate a ministry or cause before you financially give to it? Where or how would you find out such information?

7. What is something you could do right now that would demonstrate the two-handed Gospel to someone in need?

About the Author

Don Stephens is the President and Chief Executive Officer of Mercy Ships. He holds a Bachelor of Science in Religious Studies from Bethany College. Don is a recipient of the Two Hungers Award and the Religious Heritage of America Award. He is also a Paul Harris Fellow through Rotary International.

In addition to his responsibilities with Mercy Ships, Don also serves as the International Director of Relief & Development for Youth With A Mission, and is a member of the International Council for Policy and Oversight for Youth With A Mission.

Don, his wife Deyon, and their four children made their home on board the M/V *Anastasis* for ten years. They now reside near Mercy Ships' International Office in Lindale, Texas.

About Mercy Ships

Mercy Ships uses ships to bring physical and spiritual healing to the poor and needy. Since 1978, Mercy Ships has provided life-changing surgeries, dental care, medical supplies, food, seeds, construction materials, development projects, discipleship training, church planting, and a message of hope to the port cities of the world.

Mercy Ships' fleet includes the largest non-governmental hospital ship in the world and is an internationally recognized relief organization. These ships serve as the maritime arm of Youth With A Mission.

For more information about Mercy Ships, contact:

Mercy Ships, P.O. Box 2020, Lindale, Texas 75771 USA
tel. (903) 963-8341 / (800) 772-SHIP